KU-466-898

ARCHAEOLOGY
AND THE
BIBLE
An Introductory
Study

Donald J. Wiseman
and
Edwin Yamauchi

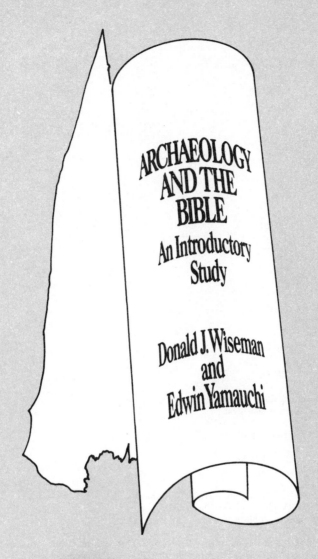

ARCHAEOLOGY AND THE BIBLE

An Introductory Study

Donald J. Wiseman
and
Edwin Yamauchi

Pickering & Inglis
LONDON · GLASGOW

CONTENTS

Preface to Archaeology and the Old Testament ...   2

Archaeology and the Old Testament
     D. J. Wiseman   3

Preface to Archaeology and the New Testament .. 62

Archaeology and the New Testament
     Edwin Yamauchi 63

Index of Contemporary Persons 110

General Index 112

Scripture Index 121

ARCHAEOLOGY AND THE OLD TESTAMENT

Preface to
Archaeology and the Old Testament

Whatever the reason that brings you to read or study the Bible—a collection of books that has had a major influence on our culture, the church, and on individuals—you may well find that you do not get far into the Old Testament without wishing to know more about its background.

For more than a century the growing science of archaeology, itself but one limited means of recovering the history of biblical times, has unearthed factual information that helps in the understanding of the peoples and places, the environment, thoughts, and actions of those days. While such extrabiblical knowledge is not essential to learning, or responding to, the message of the Bible, it does help us to bridge the gap between the historical events recorded there and today and to see how relevant and reliable the Bible is for us in the modern world.

This introduction is intended to provide an outline and overall view of the subject. It may be supplemented by reference to specialist books on archaeology, some of which are listed in the bibliographies. This book will also provide a basis on which to build the new information that will surely come to light with new work in the lands of the Bible. The section on the Old Testament was originally written in 1974-5 as an introductory study for *The Expositor's Bible Commentary*, volume 1, which was eventually published in 1979.

Donald J. Wiseman

ARCHAEOLOGY AND THE OLD TESTAMENT

Introduction

Archaeology—"the study of antiquity"—today uses all modern scientific methods to recover the material remains and meaning of the past, of ancient man and his environment. The finds include all *realia*, not merely artifacts and objects, ornaments, tools, weapons, and vessels, but also stone, metal, clay, papyri, and parchment that may have been used in building and decoration or as writing material. Archaeology usually involves the recovery by excavation of ancient places and their contents, including written documents, and provides essential data for the study of ancient history of which it is the handmaid.

Applied to the OT, biblical archaeology is the selection of the evidence for those regions, places, and periods in which the peoples of OT times lived. Critical evaluations of the results of archaeological research in the ancient Near East has contributed much to our understanding of these peoples and their manner of life. The abundant documentary evidence discovered has provided the means for us to enter at least partially into their contemporary thought. Such studies must not be expected to elucidate all problems, especially those of a nonmaterial nature. Yet they have given us illustrations and explanations of many biblical narratives, have provided extrabiblical confirmation of many details of the biblical history and have acted as a corrective to numerous erroneous interpretations.

Limitations

Archaeology is not an exact science. Therefore its results may undergo subjective selection and interpretation, though the methodology and excavation techniques are basically agreed upon among scholars of various nationalities. However, the factual evidence produced may be limited in that only a fraction of antiquity has survived or been recovered. In Palestine alone, of more than six thousand sites surveyed, fewer than two hundred have been excavated, and of these only twenty-eight to any major extent. Roughly the same proportion applies to Syria, Jordan, Iraq, and Iran but not to Egypt. Some sites are still occupied (e.g., Damascus, Jerusalem, Erbil) and can therefore be only partially examined. The precise location of some prominent OT places (e.g., OT Jericho and Ai) is still questioned. Only a fraction of the objects retrieved from some sites has been adequately published. In Palestine, the high water table may have caused its principal writing materials (papyrus and parchment) to perish. Yet, of the estimated half a million documents from OT times—mostly those on clay and sherds from outside Palestine—fewer than ten percent have as yet been published.

Dating Evidence

Only in recent decades have refined and accurate archaeological methods of stratification and typology related to local conditions and places of origin of wares enabled reliable comparisons to be made between sites and objects. The value of archaeological evidence is greatly enhanced when it can be correlated with a definite time scale. The most reliable evidence, therefore, is found in the historical periods when dateable or dated inscriptions are discovered. The most common basis of dating other finds is that of the types of pottery shapes and fabrication. For Palestine between the twelfth and sixth centuries B.C. this ceramic index is remarkably close-knit, though it may yet be proved that similar types may have been introduced by custom or as imports at varying stages. The detailed correlation of certain types of objects (e.g., lamps, seals, or weapons) or architectural features (such as houses, palaces, or gateways) with other evidence enables the history of the development of the object and its use to be read. The association of certain types of pottery or architecture with specific peoples or periods enables the archaeologist to trace transitions and cross-cultural influences. Pollen analysis and Carbon 14 dating methods have proved of particular and increasing use for assessing prehistoric periods, though the latter method still raises problems of close definition.

Inscriptions or documents may be tentatively and relatively dated according to the stage of the development of the script employed, whether it is monumental or cursive. Internal references to a known historical event or person also aid in dating. Many Sumerian and Akkadian texts are dated by year formulae (c. 2400–1600 B.C.); in Assyria, by the name of an eponym (*limmu*) official (c. 1900–620 B.C.) or in Babylonia by the regnal year of a king (c. 600–312 B.C.). Thereafter dating was by eras (e.g., Seleucid).

Methods

1. *Exploration.* Interest in the Holy Land early led travelers to record the topography and to try to identify biblical sites mainly on the basis of their location and correspondence with surviving Arabic place-names. The publications of the Americans Edward Robinson and Eli Smith after 1838 and the Swiss Tobler in 1867 were followed by the more systematic surveys made on behalf of the Palestine Exploration Fund (founded in 1865) by C.R. Condor and H.H. (later Lord) Kitchener. In the period from 1872 to 1878 this British expedition drew a map to the scale of one inch to a mile of their survey of western Palestine. In 1884/85 G. Schumacher did similar work on behalf of the American Palestine Exploration Society in northern Transjordan. In 1865 the PEF sent Charles Warren to excavate Jerusalem.

Farther afield, the Frenchman P.E. Botta had started digging in the ruins of Nineveh in 1842, to be followed there and at Calah (Nimrud) by the young Englishman A.H. Layard. W.K. Loftus worked from 1851 in the Babylonian plain at Nippur, Warka (Erech), and Ur; the French, at Susa (1854); and the Germans, at Babylon (1897–) and Asshur (1903–). So began a century of work in Mesopotamia that gave much new information about the major opponent of Israel and was of value to OT research, especially through the many cuneiform texts discovered there.

2. *Excavation*. In Palestine, the surface explorers lacked the means of dating the masonry, pottery, and other objects they discovered until Flinders Petrie, "The father of Palestinian archaeology," and P.J. Bliss, his assistant, adapted the experience they had gained in Egypt to show how the various levels of remains made by successive occupants at Tell el-Hesi in southwest Palestine in 1890 were associated with characteristic pottery types, some of which compared with dated Egyptian finds. Bliss adopted this technique when he later worked with A.C. Dickie at Jerusalem (1894–97) and with R.A.S. Macalister at Gezer (1902–09). These initial attempts, with those of G.H. Reisner at Samaria (1908–10), led to a developed method of stratigraphy that has been subject to relatively little modification since it was placed on a firm basis by the pottery chronology worked out by H. Vincent by 1918. Before World War I, excavation had also begun at Ta'anach, Megiddo, and Jericho.

Between the wars, W.F. Albright worked at Tell Beit Mirsim, once thought to be the biblical Debir or Kirjath-Sephir (1906–32). The Americans at Megiddo (1929–38) planned to excavate the site completely, but because it covered thirteen acres, the task was impossible. Garstang's work at Jericho (1930–36) has in part to be reappraised following the continuation of work there by I. Kenyon (1952–58), who used more-developed techniques. Other noteworthy work was carried out at Tell el-Husn (Beth-shan), Sebastiyeh (Samaria), Tell Duweir (Lachish), Et-Tell (Ai?), Tell el-Fûl (Gibeah), Beitin (Beth-el), Balatah (Shechem), Tell Seilun (Shiloh), Tell el-Kheleifeh (Ezion-geber), and Jerusalem. Work at many of these same sites resumed after World War II, with the important addition of Tell el-Far'ah (Tirzah), Tell Qasileh, Dibhan (Dibon), Tell Dotha (Dothan), Tell el-Qedar (Hazor), Tell el-Jîb (Gibeon), Tell Sheikh el-Areini, Qumrān, and Masada. A list of over two hundred Palestinian sites, with the dates they were excavated and primary publication references, is given in Eleanor K. Vogel, *Bibliography of Holy Land Sites* (Cincinnati: Hebrew Union College, 1972).

In Syria the excavations at Ras Shamra (Ugarit), At-shanah (Alalah), and Tell Hariri (Mari) have done much to increase our knowledge of OT times. The same applies to the continued work in the major cities of Mesopotamia at Nineveh, Nimrud (Calah of Gen 10:11–12), Asshur, Nuzi, Nippur, Warka, and Ur, among others, and at Ammān (Jordan) and Buseirah in Edom.

Classification of Archaeological Periods

The various levels or periods of occupation are commonly designated by archaeologists in the manner indicated in the table on pages 10–13, which also notes some of the alternative nomenclature sometimes used.

Archaeology and the OT periods

Prehistory

A sequence of Palaeolithic remains from the Carmel caves (Wadi al-Mugharah), 'Eron and 'Oren, with a gap in the Upper Palaeolithic-Mesolithic stages, gives evidence of food gathering and an early association with prehistoric Europe rather than with Africa. This is supported by the Middle Palaeolithic inhabitants' close relationship physically to the European Neanderthal race. A flint industry is associated with the Natufians when in Mesolithic times there is evidence for the beginning of settlement, agriculture, and domestication of animals. Neolithic sites are found in Yarmuk and Sha'ar Haggolan (Galilee) about the same time as those in the Nile, Cyprus (Khirokitia), and the Tigris valley (Jarmo). At Jericho a prepottery people (c. 7500 B.C.) made massive defenses as well as remarkable plastered skulls and figurines, the purpose of which is as yet unknown.

In the Chalcolithic period, painted pottery, polychrome wall paintings, and simple copper axeheads are traced in the Jordan valley, Telulat Ghassul, Esdraelon, northern Negeb, and near Gaza. Metal appears to have been in widespread use. Clay models show that curved vaulted roofs were being incorporated into houses and underground stores (Abu Matar), and rock cisterns for water supply are now found for the first time. The transition from the fourth millennium agricultural communities at Ghassul in the Jordan valley and at other Palestinian sites to the Early Bronze Age is still ill-defined.

In 1974 to 1976 excavations at Tell Mardikh (ancient Ebla, south of Aleppo in northern Syria) uncovered about 15,000 clay tablets inscribed in the cuneiform script with an early NW Semitic dialect of c. 2300 B.C.—the time of the Babylonian king Naram-Sin (equated by some with Nimrod of Gen 10:9) who campaigned in the area. The texts include parts of the Epic of Gilgamesh, which includes the Babylonian accounts of the Flood, the epic of

ARCHAEOLOGY AND OLD TESTAMENT TIMES

Approx. Date B.C.	Palestine/Syria/Jordan	Also called
I. *Prehistoric*		
–8000	Paleolithic	(Old) Stone Age
8000–6000	Mesolithic	Middle Stone Age
		Natufian
		Tahunian/Jerichoan
6000–4000	Neolithic	Prepottery N.
		Pottery N. (5000–)
4000–3200	Chalcolithic	Ghassulian (end)
3200–3000	Esdraelon	
II. *Bronze Age*		
3000–2800	Early Bronze (Age) I (= EB)	Early Canaanite (= EC)
2800–2600	EB II	
2600–2300	EB III	
2300–2200	EB IV	EB IIIb
2200–1950	Intermediate Bronze (= IB)	EB-MB
		MB I/MCI
1950–1750	Middle Bronze (= MB) I	Middle Canaanite (= MC) IIa
1750–1600	MB IIa	MB/MC IIb
1600–1550	MB IIb	MB/MC IIc
1550–1400	Late Bronze (= LB) I	Late Canaanite (= LC) I
1400–1300	LB IIa	LC IIa
1300–1200	LB IIc	LC IIc

Assyria/Babylonia	Egypt
'Ubaid	Prehistoric
Uruk	Tasian
Proto-Literate	Badarian
	Naqada I–II
Early Dynastic (= ED) I	Pre-Dynastic I
ED II	Archaic Period
	Dyn. I–III
ED III	Old Kingdom
	Dyn. III–IV
Sargonid	Dyn. V–VI
Ur III	First Intermediate
	Period
Early Old Babylonian	Dyn. VII–XI
	Middle Kingdom (XII)
Late Old Babylonian	Second Intermediate
	Dyn. XIII–XVII
Kassite	
Middle Assyrian	New Kingdom (XVIII–)
Middle Babylonian	
	Dyn. XIX

11

ARCHAEOLOGY AND OLD TESTAMENT TIMES

Approx. Date B.C.	Palestine/Syria/Jordan	Also called
III. *Iron Age*		
1200–1150	Iron (Age) Ia (= I)	(Early) Israelite Early Iron (= EI) I
1150–1025	Ib	
1025–950	Ic	EI II
950–900	Id	
900–800	IIa	Middle Iron Middle Israelite (= MI) I Israelite II (970–840)
800–700	IIb	
700–600	IIc	MI II Israelite III (840–580)
600–330	III	Late Iron Late Israelite (= LI) Israelite IV Persian
IV. *Hellenistic Age*		
330–165	Hellenistic I	
165–63	Hellenistic II	Hellenistic-Herodian Maccabean
63–A.D.70	Hellenistic-Roman	

12

Assyria/Babylonia	Egypt
	Dyn. **XX**
	Late Period
Neo-Assyrian	Dyn. **XXI**
	Dyn. **XXII** (Libyan)
	Dyn. **XXIII–XXV**
	Dyn. **XXVI** (Saite)
Neo-Babylonian	Dyn. **XXVII–**
(Chaldean)	
Hellenistic	Hellenistic Egypt
	Dyn. **XXVIII–XXX**
	Roman

creation, the Babylonian "Job," literary, historical, administrative, and school texts of a type well known in later Syria (Ugarit). They thus attest an early literary tradition as already previously well known from Babylonia. New light is now thrown on the kingdom of Ebrum (cf. Eber of Gen 10:21) who had Duddiya as his vassal in Assyria (Ashur). The latter, as Tudia, is mentioned in the early genealogy heading the Assyrian King List as one of their ancestors "who lived in tents." He was assumed to be a "fictitious" eponymous ancestor.

The texts mention Cyprus, Mesopotamia (Erbil), Palestine, and Canaan, as well as Hazor, Lachish, Gezer, Dor, Megiddo, and possibly Urusalem (Jerusalem) and Sinai. The naming of such individuals as Abarama and Isma'el, names that occur elsewhere in the ancient Near East, is not a direct reference to the later biblical characters of the name. At this time Syro-Palestine seems to have been the home of many nomadic groups. Further research on these texts will undoubtedly show much more of the history and culture of a period and place hitherto little known but adjacent to Amorite homelands. It should, moreover, counter the prevalent tendency of some scholars to belittle the reliability of the patriarchal narratives.

Early Bronze Age (EB I) settlements develop into towns at a number of sites. At first they were unwalled, as Megiddo (excavation level XIX), Beth-shan (XVII–XVI), Tell Shuneh (II–III), and Arad (IV), but later towns are walled, with gateways (Tell el-Far'ah, Gath), the mud-brick sometimes reinforced with stone. There is therefore a marked continuity from fully occupied open village to large walled town. The building of walls may be due to influence from Egypt and Sumer or to a growing intercity rivalry, though the latter is denied by some archaeologists.[1] At this time the pottery in the north (Beth-Yerah II, Beth-shan XI) differs from the contemporary wares in the south at Jerusalem (Ophel), Gezer, Ai, Jericho (VI–VII), and Tell en-Nasbeh where a strong Egyptian influence can be traced (e.g., Jericho IV). The northern towns flourished and new pottery techniques (Khirbet Kerak) and architectural developments show a flourishing community. The developments include town walls and citadel and temple layout in which the holy of holies is approached directly via an outer court (Ai, EB III). The earliest towns often contained well-built rectangular houses, sometimes with roofs supported by rows of pillars (Tell el-Far'ah) and with well-constructed silos for grain storage (Jericho). These developments are not surprising and can be matched at the even larger complexes already long-established in southern Babylonia at Erech (Warka), Nippur, Ur, Lagash, and Eridu and reflected in Genesis 5 and 10. There, from a period long before the Early Bronze Age in Palestine, the first written documents have been found. Written in this period (c. 2700 B.C.), texts with a wide range of Semitic literature already showing a lengthy literary development have been discovered at Abu Salabikh, Fara, and other early Babylonian sites.

Nomadic Incursions

The break with the Early Bronze Age is marked by violent destruction of the towns (e.g., Jericho). Kenyon and others have associated this with the incursions of the Amorite nomads. But these peoples, only seminomads,

---

[1]P. Lapp in *Near Eastern Archaeology in the Twentieth Century*, ed. James A. Sanders Garden City, N.Y.: Doubleday and Co., Inc., 1970], pp. 111ff.; cf. R. Amiran ibid., pp. 83ff.

had moved much earlier into Syria and Babylonia according to Liverani.[2] There is as yet little justification for identifying the population of the Early Bronze–Middle Bronze Age, with their distinctive pottery and weapon styles and lack of substantial buildings, exclusively with Amorite tribesmen. Certainly the rich tomb groups from Jericho, Tell el-'Ajjûl, and Megiddo, showing individual or double burials with personal possessions in rock-hewn tombs, are in marked contrast with the communal burials of the earlier period. The median chronology for these is given by objects from the Megiddo tombs that compare with similar types found at Ras Shamra and Mesopotamia and dated c. 2200–2000 B.C.

Just before 1900 B.C., a new civilization emerged that was to dominate Palestine without any apparent break for seven hundred years. These peoples, coming mainly from Syria and Phoenicia, brought with them a new type of wheel-made pottery. Once more the incursions appear to have been gradual and can be traced at Megiddo, Tell Beit Mirsim, and Tell el-'Ajjûl. Egyptian execration texts show that Palestine and Transjordan were still occupied by seminomads who controlled the areas between the Canaanite cities that were once more expanding on their earlier sites.

The Patriarchal Age (c. 1950–1750 B.C.)

The Patriarchs fit best into the early Middle Bronze Age (MBA I), though their association with the Amorites or other folk-movements (including early Hapiru) known from contemporary texts cannot be proved. The Genesis narrative accords well with the archaeologically known

---

[2]D.J. Wiseman, ed., *Peoples of Old Testament Times* (Oxford: Clarendon Press, 1973), p. 109.

occupation of the city-states that were then a dominant feature of Palestine. The occupation of Bethel, Shechem, Hebron (Kirjath-Arba), and the Dead Sea region of Sodom and Gomorrah is confirmed, as is that of the Negeb in southwest Palestine where flocks and herds (cf. Gen. 18:7; 20:1; 24:62) and grain crops (Gen 26:12; 37:7) are traced in MBA I. There is valuable evidence of the verisimilitude of the patriarchal personal and place names at this time. Thus, the name "Abram" occurs in a text from Dilbat (*Aba[m]rama*) and Aburahana (Abraham) and Zabilan (Zebulon) in Egyptian execration texts. Turahi (Terah), Nahur (Nahor), Sarugi (Serug), Laban, and Mar(Ben)-Yamin (Benjamin) are in eighteenth-century texts from Mari with reference to the Harran area and Ya'qub-il (Jacob) from nearby Chagar-Bazar. Other texts' from these towns and from Alalah (from the eighteenth to the fifteenth century), Ur, Ras Shamra (fourteenth century), and Nuzi in Assyria (fifteenth century) throw considerable light on the patriarchal social customs. It can be seen that it was usual for a childless couple to adopt an heir and then displace him in the event of the birth of a real son (Gen 15:4). According to her marriage contract, a barren woman was to provide her husband with a slave-girl to bear a son. Marriages were arranged for public purposes by the rulers of Ugarit and Qatna, as well as by Egyptian kings, and this may be reflected in the adventures of Sarah (Gen 20) and Rebekah (Gen 26). The special position of the first-born son (cf. Gen 21:10ff.; 48:14ff.), the bridegroom "asking" for a daughter as bride, the use of betrothal and bride-gifts (Gen 34:12), and the stipulation of marriage-contracts that a man might take a third wife only if the first two were barren or take a second wife only if the first failed to give birth within seven years explain incidents in Genesis (e.g., 29:

18,27: Jacob's possible need to wait seven years for Rachel). Nuzi texts refer to a man's transferring his inheritance for three sheep and uphold the validity of an oral blessing as a deathbed will. The type of sale contract involved in the purchase of the cave of Machpelah (Gen 23) is similar to both Old Babylonian and Hittite legal texts of this period.

From a study of the Mari texts, it is evident that an incident like that related in Genesis 14, in which Amraphel (not the same name as Hammurapi), Arioch (Arriwuk occurs only at this time), and Tidal (Tudhalia) were opposed by Abraham and his armed retainers (*hanîkîm,* a word otherwise found only in Egyptian texts of the nineteenth to eighteenth centuries B.C.) could likely have taken place only in this period, which, according to the Mari letters, was one in which such coalitions were formed.

Camel bones from Mari c. 2500; representations on seals, plaques, and figurines from Byblos, Babylonia, and Egypt; and references in Sumerian and Babylonian texts show that the citing of camels in Abraham's time is no anachronism. At that time camels were ridden behind the hump and, with donkeys, were used as slow-moving beasts of burden, though their major domestication and use in war did not occur until c. 1500–1250 B.C.

The Late Bronze Age

About 1700 B.C. a strengthening and enlargement of the massive defenses of walled cities can be seen in the addition of a steep slope of stone or beaten earth with a smooth plastered face held at its base by a retaining wall (glacis). This can be traced in Syria (Carchemish and Qatna), Palestine (Hazor), Dan (Laish), Shechem, Tirzah, Old Gaza, Tell el-Far'ah (Sharuhen), Tell el-Ajjûl, Ashkelon, Tell Beit Mirsim (Tell Jerisheh), and in Egypt at Tell el-

Yahudiyeh. The construction of these is generally attributed to the Hyksos who seem to combine non-Semitic elements (Horites-Hurrians) with Semites (Amorites). These people, pressed southwest by the rising Hittite and Kassite powers, overthrew the native rulers of Egypt c. 1720. Their success was in part due to the use of chariots and horses (skeletons of which were found at Tell el-'Ajjûl) and to their organizational ability that led to the rise of strong local rulers, each major city having its own monarch. The nobility lived in well-built mansions that contrasted with the much humbler dwellings around them. Middle Bronze IIC tombs bear witness to the wealth of this period and numerous scarabs to the many sealed documents current within a domain stretching from the Euphrates to the Nile. This was an important period and later Hebrews were to marvel at the massive defenses (Num 13:28), meet the feudal type of monarchy in Palestine (1 Sam 27:6), and themselves desire a similar system (1 Sam 8:11–18).

In Egypt the Joseph history (Gen 37–50) fits well into the late Middle Kingdom (Dynasty XIII) and Hyksos period. The Wilbur papyri (c. 1740 B.C.) shows in a list of one hundred slaves that more than half were "Asiatics," i.e., Semites from Palestine, among them 'š-ra (Asher) and šp-ra (cf. Shiphra, Exod 1:15). Some of these rose to higher positions and some were domestic servants. The twenty silver shekels paid for Joseph (Gen 37:28) was the average slave price for the eighteenth century, whereas later the price rose until by the fifteenth to fourteenth centuries it was from forty to fifty shekels. A Ras Shamra text (RS 20.21) tells of a man in southern Syria who was sold by his companion to passing Egyptians, who, however, abandoned him, taking only his goods. The use of contemporarily attested technical terms (e.g., "butler,"

19

"baker" as courtiers [*saris*]), the prison procedure, and proper names, parallels with the Egyptian *Tale of Two Brothers:* the court etiquette (Gen 41:14), the investiture, and economic milieu all bear witness to the validity of the Joseph narratives. The fact that some Egyptian names (Potiphar, Asenath, Zaphenath-Paneah) are not attested in texts till the twelfth to tenth centuries B.C. could be due to the sparsity of earlier documentary evidence rather than to the proposal that modern subsitutes were inserted during the transmission of the text.[3]

The Hyksos empire seems to have broken up quickly following their expulsion from Egypt in the third quarter of the sixteenth century. The Egyptians harried them into Canaan, as illustrated by their local tomb paintings of the siege of Sharuhen and by the destruction levels at Tell Beit Mirsim, Beth-zur, Jericho, and Megiddo. The subsequent Late Bronze Age is well illustrated by the correspondence between the city-rulers and their allies and their overlords in the fourteenth to thirteenth centuries (The Amarna letters and cuneiform text from Ugarit). Here, as in the earlier Middle Bronze Age, seminomads including (H)apiru moved in between the towns amid the uncertain situation caused by the growing weakness of Egyptian control. Despite some evidence of trade with Egypt, Cyprus, and Mesopotamia in the jewelry hoards from Tell-el-'Ajjûl tombs near Gaza and Megiddo, the hill towns were poorer than their coastal counterparts in Phoenicia and Syria. Art forms on cylinder seals, pots, and stelae show a mixed Egyptian and Mesopotamian (thus possibly local Canaanite) predominance with purely

---

[3]So J. Vergote, *Joseph en Egypte* (Louvain: Publications Un Universitaires, 1959-Orientalia et Biblica Louvaniensia 3), pp.147, 148.

Egyptian stelae and statues set up in places where they dominated (Beth-shan, Chinnereth).

1. *The Exodus.* The end of the Late Bronze Age in Palestine is marked by several destruction levels, some of which have been ascribed to the suppression of rebellion by the Egyptians. So Tell el-Hesi (Eglon?) was destroyed four times and Megiddo and Beth-shan twice by the end of the thirteenth century. The ruin of Tell Beit Mirsim and the contemporary occupation at Jericho is now ascribed to the fourteenth century, not the fifteenth as at one time supposed. The fallen walls at the latter city, taken by Garstang to be evidence of a destruction c. 1407 B.C., are now dated by Kenyon to the Early Bronze Age, though there is evidence of the abandonment of Jericho c. 1325. The now evident destruction of Lachish, Tell Beit Mirsim, and Ashdod (Judg 1:18) may relate to attacks by the incoming Hebrews, and the excavators attribute the burning of Hazor (XIII) to Joshua's attack (Josh 11). Those who argue for the earlier date of the conquest have to assign these thirteenth-century destructions to the Philistines, the Judges, or some other cause. They rightly point out that only Hazor, Ai, and Jericho are said in the Old Testament to have been burned and that there is possibly some archaeological evidence for this in the Late Bronze IIA levels there.[4] They also explain the reference to Ra'amses in Exodus 1:11, as reference to an eighteenth-dynasty Rameses,[5] or as a substitution of a later for an earlier name. Pithom and Ra'amses (probably Pi-Rammsē of Egyptian texts) were founded by Sethos I and mainly built

---

[4]Bruce K. Waltke, BS 129 (1972): 33–47.
[5]Gleason L. Archer, JETS 17 (1974): 49, 50.

by Rameses II (1304–). The latter city is identified with Tanis or, more likely, Qantir.

Surveys by Glueck and others showed that Edom, Moab, and Ammon, who opposed Moses, were not settled to any great extent till the thirteenth century, though this may have to be modified by some recent findings in Jordan.[6] There is somewhat clearer evidence for the first mention of "Israel" in Palestine on the Merenptah stela at Lachish dated 1224 B.C., which names places and peoples that Egyptian kings claimed to have subdued. A stela of Seti I from Beth Shan dated 1313 names the "Apiru of the mountains of Yarmuth."

The main difference between proponents of the early (c. 1440 B.C.) and late date (c. 1270) for the Exodus lies in the interpretation of 1 Kings 6:1, which states that it was 480 years from the time the Israelites left Egypt to the founding of Solomon's temple in c. 960 B.C. Unger and Archer believe that this demands the earlier date.[7] On the other hand, Kitchen and other evangelicals argue that, since the archaeological evidence does not seem to support such a date, the 480 years may be the total of regnal years that may have in part been concurrent, as commonly occurs in Mesopotamian and Egyptian king lists (e.g., Turin Papyrus for Dynasties XIII to XVII; it gives a total of 450 years of reigns that are partly overlapping and known from other sources to have occupied a total of c. 240 years). The biblical account of the Judges does the same.

---

[6] *Vetus Testamentum* 21 (1971): 199–123.
[7] Leon J. Wood, "The Date of the Exodus" in *New Perspectives on the OT*, ed. J.B. Payne (Waco: Word Books, 1970).

2. *The Sinai covenant.* The covenant made by God with his people at Sinai is at the heart of the OT and is unique. Nothing similar and no covenant direct from any god to man is found among ancient Near Eastern texts or any with purely moral subject matter. The literary form, however, may be compared with the international treaties of the fourteenth to thirteenth centuries known from Hittite sources but themselves based on a Mesopotamian style of text already attested and used in the fifteenth century (Alalah) and earlier. The scheme of these texts, which followed the oral deposition and oath at a solemn assembly, is as follows: (1) Preamble, or title, indicating the author (cf. Deut 1:1–5); (2) historical prologue, which may be stated (Deut 1:6–3:29), summarized (Exod 20:2), or assumed from the circumstances of the ceremony (as in the Esarhaddon Assyrian treaties of 627 B.C.); (3) detailed stipulations laying obligations on the vassal in the form "You shall (not) . . ." (cf. Exod 20–31); (4) ultimate deposition of the document (Deut 10:1–5; Exod 25:16) and arrangements for the periodic public reading of the terms and for their teaching to succeeding generations (Deut 31:10–13); (5) witnesses that are usually gods, but since the Lord swears only by himself, the only witnesses at Sinai are heaven and earth; and (6) curses and blessings on the vassal who breaks or keeps the terms of the treaty. Some of these were demonstrated. Note that Deuteronomy 28 has the reverse order of blessings before curses.

In these cuneiform and Aramaic texts (Bar-Ga'yah and Mati-el of the eighth century) the order of some sections may be varied or some omitted or recorded on a separate document. The discovery of these texts shows that such treaty/covenant law was the essential basis of all state, interstate, and interpersonal law and contract throughout the ancient Near East. It has recently given rise to a fresh study of covenant terminology both within and outside the OT.[8]

3. *Writing.* The cuneiform script used in Mesopotamia since c. 3500 B.C. was taught in scribal schools in Syria (Mari. c. 2400) and Anatolia also. At Alalah, an agricultural town in Syria, at least six scribes were at work at one time writing historiographic, legal, and economic texts in addition to the usual correspondence, administrative, recording, and school exercises. By the thirteenth century B.C. scribes at Ras Shamra (Ugarit) were using the Akkadian cuneiform script for all these same purposes alongside texts written in the local Semitic dialect, Hurrian, Hittite, Sumerian, and a simplified cuneiform alphabetic script used primarily for religious epics, according to extant texts in Ugaritic. The scribes wrote a number of literary compositions, including a Semitic version of the *Epic of Gilgamesh,* of which a fragment from the fifteenth century has also been found at Megiddo. Among other tablets was a local version of the "Babylonian Job," discussing the problem of suffering. The presence of this tablet indicates an earlier date for the origin of this type of literature and so of its biblical counterpart than some critics would normally allow. There are proverbs and other wisdom literature similar in genre to those in the OT. In the following century, tablets using the cuneiform script originate in Palestine (e.g., Amarna letters, Ta'anach, Megiddo, Jericho, Shechem, Gezer, Hazor, and Tell el-Hesi).

By the Late Middle Bronze Age the Semitic alphabet, perhaps developed under the use of the Egyptian hiero-

---

[8]E.g., M. Weinfeld, "Covenant Terminology" in *Journal of the American Oriental Society* 93 (1973): 190–199.

glyphs for writing foreign names, was already in use in Sinai (Serabit el-Khadem) and, in another form, soon thereafter in Byblos. By 1500 B.C. similar inscriptions, but now losing their original pictographic form, are found in Palestine at Gezer, Shechem (plaque), and Lachish (inscribed dagger). Well before the end of the second millennium the pressures of trade and need for communication led to the widespread use of this simple form of writing (e.g., in marking personal objects; cf. stone inscriptions of Ahiram). Thus, by the time of the entry of the Hebrews into Canaan in the Late Bronze Age they would be confronted, if not already familiar, with at least five different forms of writing systems used for eight or more languages: (1) Egyptian hieroglyphs (Beth-shan, Chinnereth); (2) the Byblos syllabic script; (3) "Proto-Hebrew" (Lachish, Hazor); (4) Akkadian (Mesopotamian) cuneiform; and (5) the Ugaritic alphabetic script (found also at Beth-Shemesh). Since at this same time the Egyptian Wen-Amun writes of taking papyrus scrolls in quantity to Byblos, we must assume that the hazards of climate and survival have so far prevented the recovery of many texts from Palestine itself in any period.

One use of these scripts is commonly found in the manufacture of stamp seals, which may have the name of the owner and perhaps also the name of his father and the title of his profession. Vattioni has listed more than 260 Hebrew seals with inscriptions in the alphabetic script, or impressions from them dated mainly to the ninth to the sixth centuries.[9] Old Testament names on these seals include those of King Jotham (2 Kings 15:30ff.); Gealiyah son of the king, probably a descendant of Jehoiakim (1 Chron 3:22); Shema‘, servant of Jeroboam; Jaazaniah,

---

[9] *Biblica* 50 (1969): 357–388; *Augustinianum* 11 1971, pp.447–454.

servant of the king (cf. 2 Kings 25:23); and Gedaliah "who is over the house" (cf. 2 Kings 18:18; NBD 1153–5).

4. *Religious architecture*. The Late Bronze Age has left remains of religious structures—temples and sanctuaries—several rebuilt on the same foundations over successive centuries as at Lachish (1500–1230 B.C.) and Megiddo. Most temples were small, but those at Beth-shan, Beersheba, and Tell el-Far'ah consisted of an anteroom and an inner room or covered niche, where the divine image or symbol rested. This was the traditional form of religious architecture throughout the ancient Near East. At Hazor a large temple had a porch added as in the later temple of Solomon. Massive walls surrounded a single room, the roof of which was supported by pillars and entered by the portico. It seems that some shrines at Middle Bronze Age Hazor, Megiddo, and Shechem had upper rooms similar to those depicted in the model temples used as incense burners. There is evidence here and at Megiddo and Shechem of the Middle Bronze Age, such as in the model temples used as incense burners, that there was an upper room in these "tower" shrines. This form was succeeded by the more conventional temple, as found at Ugarit and Alalah in Syria, where the antechamber is smaller than the holy place and was entered from the long side. Square temples of the Late Bronze Age are known from Shechem (Mount Gerizim) and Amman, but the former does not have evidence of cremated human beings as foundation deposits such as is found at the latter (cf. Josh 6:26).

The numerous small male and female metal and clay figurines (MBA-LBA), some skirted or holding weapons —figurines that have commonly been identified with Baals or Astarte—have not always been found in sacred buildings. So they may be amulets, charms, or votive objects, much like the many pottery plaques and figures of a naked female (the goddess Asherah?) found in this and earlier periods in Palestine as well as in Mesopotamia. The biblical account of Canaanite religious practices and of the actual deities in the pantheon can be checked from the bilingual lists from Ras Shamra. In these lists Ba'al Sapon, the Baal of the heights, is followed by "the god of the fathers" (*il abi*, sometimes wrongly interpreted as "god the spirit"). Then the god Dagan (*ilDagan*) is followed in the list by seven Baals. The banal antics of some of these deities portrayed in the thirteenth-century Ugaritic epics contrast with the high expressions of devotion found in some other contemporary texts.

At Gezer and other sites, standing stones (as later found also at Hazor) probably indicate a mortuary shrine. Hill shrines or "high places," common in the following centuries and known best from the Nabatean high place at Petra, can be traced only with difficulty, because most archaeological effort is directed to a town or its neighboring built-up areas. Such high places could be built of stones or earth to represent a mound, as at Megiddo in the Early Bronze Age, Naharayah near Haifa (Middle Bronze II), and Hazor in the Late Bronze Age. The earliest of such high places may show impregnation with the oil used in pouring libations on the site. Later Israelite high places included open-air shrines approached by a flight of wide stone and brick steps, as at Tel Dan.[10]

The Monarchy (Iron Age)

1. *Philistia.* The Amarna correspondence and Ugarit texts of the fourteenth century already show that Ashdod

---

[10]*The Biblical Archaeologist* 37 (1974): 40–43.

and Ashkelon (under a non-Semitic ruler Widiya) were influential trade centres and that Gath, Gaza, and Joppa were independent towns. Raiders and settlers from Cyprus joined other sea peoples already settled on the Palestinian coast. There is therefore no reason to think of patriarchal relations with the "Philistines" as an anachronism. Aegean contacts continued into the thirteenth century, as shown by pottery finds at Ashkelon, Tell el-Hesi, Tell el-'Ajjûl, and Tell el-Far'ah and by Cretan seals found near Gaza. In the twelfth century, a new style of pottery, combining elements from Cyprus (Late Helladic III) with local Egyptian and Palestinian, appears. This is generally designated "Philistinian," since it is found at Gaza, Ashkelon, Ashdod, and in their rich hinterland—the area known to have been occupied by these people in the twelfth century. They mainly appear to have taken over older sites in Southwest Canaan by conquest, though some new foundations (Qasileh and Khirbet el Muqanna') are attributed to them.

The Philistines, possibly the "Egyp(tian). *Prst*" and their associated Tjekker colonists depicted on the Egyptian wall paintings of the tomb of Rameses III (1198–1166) at Medinet Habu, soon settled in southwest Palestine. Their arrival marks a destruction level that puts an end to the Late Bronze Age at cities in the coastal plain. Their characteristic feathered headdresses and weapons (some were found near Jaffa) associate them with peoples of a northern or Caucasian origin. While a number of clay anthropoid coffins found at Beth-shan and Lachish may be Philistinian, their presence there may be due to later trading. More certain evidence of Philistinian settlement is their painted pottery with its distinctive decorations and geometric and bird patterns found at Sharuhen, Gerar, as far north as Joppa, throughout the Shephelah, and from Debir to Gezer. Trade can account for these wares as far inland as Deir 'Alla in the Jordan valley, but only after an interval. Thus the biblical accent on the pentapolis centered on Gaza, Ashkelon, Gath (Tell el-'Areini or Tell en-Najila?), and Ekron is confirmed. But the extension and comparison of their form of rule under a lord (*seren*, Gk. "tyrant") to the Israelite amphyctyony is increasingly to be doubted.

A temple at Tell Qasileh is the only Philistinian temple so far excavated (by Mazar in 1972). This had a structure basically different from Canaanite temples and Solomon's later construction. Two central pillars were the sole support for the roof, an architectural design that may throw light on Samson's action in pulling down the Gaza temple single-handedly (Judg 16:29, 30). The contrast between the well-drained foundations of the Canaanites and Philistines and the cruder Israelite habitations in the time of the Judges (e.g., at Bethel) is clear. Where the latter built on or occupied earlier property, they kept to the ground plan but used primarily only the ground floor. Few repairs were made and this may indicate that there was a lack of coordination with work in gangs at the larger sites.

The period of expansion brought the Philistines into contact with the Hebrews in c. 1100 B.C., first in the Southwest between Timnah and Ekron (Judg 3:31; 14:4), where they were a much-feared enemy (Judg 14:11, 12), and later at Shiloh. Their failure to penetrate farther against the united resistance of Judah under David is attested by the almost complete absence of evidence for any settlement, with some possible traces of trade at Gibeah, Jerusalem, Beth-zur, and Tell en-Nasbeh. The Philistines were not the first to develop the use of iron, which is found from the fourteenth century as a Hittite exploitation. A Tell el-Fara'ah tomb yields the earliest iron dagger and knife from Palestine, and the Israelites found it hard to break the Philistine monopoly in tempering iron and their consequent economic superiority (1 Sam 13:18–22). In the early monarchy, iron finally displaces copper and bronze for ploughshares and sickles.

2. *The united monarchy.* Israel gradually took over something of the technical ability of the Philistines who dominated the plains, while Saul and David consolidated their position in the hills. At Saul's hometown and capital, Gibeah (Tell el-Fûl), the earliest Israelite iron implements were already in use, and soon thereafter iron axes, mattocks, plow-points, hooks, and sickles lead to improvement in agricultural methods and to an industrial revolution. Iron nails are now found in construction work (cf. 1 Chron 22:3). Whereas previously the Israelites had not been able to contain the Canaanite chariotry easily or to drive out their settled communities, now their own population increased and they were able to construct the vital wells and cisterns in places previously ill-watered.

The oldest dateable Israelite fortification is at Gibeah (IA I), three miles north of Jerusalem, excavated by W.F. Albright in 1923–33. A corner tower and adjacent massive casemate walls of a type traceable to the time of Abimelech at Tell Beit Mirsim and Beth-shemesh, formed a rudimentary palace-fortress. This building was soon destroyed by fire, perhaps after the battle of Michmash (1 Sam 13–14) and then rebuilt. Others interpret this as the place from which Saul and Jonathan drove out the Philistines (1 Sam 13:3). Shiloh (Khirbet Seilûn) reveals no direct evidence of the actual resting place of the ark of the covenant. Shiloh was certainly occupied in the early Iron Age (c. 1200–1000) and was destroyed soon thereafter by the Philistines (as Jer 7:12 recalls). The layout of a later Byzantine church there follows the pattern of the tabernacle. The cultural standard gradually improved, but little remains of the time of David unless the Jebusite glacis and part of the wall of Ophel, the new "city of David," can be attributed to him. The old Warren's shaft leading to Gihon ("Gusher") in the Kidron valley outside the city walls discovered in 1867 follows the line of an earlier Canaanite tunnel for bringing water into the city. This is generally considered to be the water course up which Joab and his men entered the city to capture it (2 Sam 5:6–8). Similar water shafts have been cleared at Gezer, Gibeon, and Hazor, and other tunnels for bringing water into a city from external springs have been found at Megiddo and elsewhere. The repair of the casemate walls at Beth Shemesh (and of the governor's residence there) and at Tell Beit Mirsim may represent action taken during David's reign to protect his territories against the Philistines.

David's organization of army leaders, personal bodyguard, priests, state archivist, and secretary, and his employment of twelve divisions taking turns at military duties, as well as of officials responsible for keeping accounts of the primary imports and exports of livestock, grain, oil, and wine, can be compared with similar arrangements revealed in texts from Ugarit and Alalah. From the latter and from Mari texts it can be shown that David's act of cutting off the hem of Saul's garment was tantamount to rebellion or freedom from a royal overlord, just as the act of seizing the hem of a king's robe denoted subordination. Although no copies of psalms from Judah have been found earlier than the Qumran texts, there are many parallels from the twelfth century and later Akkadian texts. These show that such compositions were easily and freely made, so that the attribution psalms to David would be in keeping with this. All the musical instruments mentioned in the Psalms are known from excavations or references before the e ighth century. A vase from Megiddo dated c. 1000 B.C. depicts a man playing a lyre. Mazar thinks that an inscribed javelin head from El-Khadr, between Bethlehem and Hebron, may have belonged to a soldier following David into exile.

3. *The age of Solomon.* The second phase of the Iron Age shows an increase in the use of iron and improvements in building techniques. Yadin's discovery of a governor's palace and an administrative building of this period and of a monumental six-roomed gateway associated with casemate walls at Hazor is of importance. By a careful reinvestigation and redating of similar structures at Megiddo and Gezer, he has shown that all these were truly Solomon's work (1 Kings 9:15). At this same time the palace-fortress, defenses, and administrative quarters at Megiddo were enlarged, using the new solid bonded masonry techniques that began to displace the casemate type of constructions, perhaps under Phoenician influence. The so-called "stables" of Solomon found there (Level IV) have since been reinterpreted to be an administrative building of the days of Ahab. The Solomonic level may well remain unexcavated beneath. Similar storerooms have been unearthed at Tell el-Hesi and Ta'anach.

In Jerusalem, Solomon built his own central palace, as well as buildings elsewhere, apparently modeled on the lines of Syrian Late Bronze Age buildings already known from Alalah and Ugarit and popular in the Iron Age. Examples of these grandiose constructions with columned portico or entrance hall (Akkad. *bīt-hilāni*) are now known from Zincirli, Tell Halaf (biblical Gozan), Tainat, and

Karatepe, and from the Assyrian bas-reliefs. The first temple used current architectural motifs and design technology. The construction of walls with layers of wood between the stone courses is known from Tainat and Alalah in Syria. Drawings on Syrian ivories illustrate cherubim (a pair of human-headed winged lions), palmettos, and lotus flowers. Lavers with pomegranate fringes have been found at Ras Shamra. The twin freestanding pillars in front of the temple have parallels elsewhere in the Near East. Solomon's work in the city may be marked by the casemate wall, blocks of stone worked by Phoenician craftsmen, and a proto-Ionic capital found in the north of Ophel. Kenyon considers the "Fill" (Millo) rebuilt by both David and Solomon to be the walled terraces on the slopes of Ophel, which needed, and show, frequent repair. The grand feast given on completion of the construction of the temple (1 Kings 8:65) is similar to that of King Ashurnasirpal II of Assyria, who describes in detail the provisions for his entertainment of 69,574 people for ten days to celebrate the opening of his new city and temple at Calah in 879 B.C.

The wealth needed for this activity was generated by the trading activity of the age. Evidence for the expeditions to Ophir (possibly [S]upara north of Bombay) is found in an inscribed potsherd from Tell Qasileh—"gold from Ophir for Beth Horon, thirty shekels." The buildings found by Glueck at the port of Tell el Kheleifeh (Ezion-geber or Elat) and once thought to be a foundry of Solomon are now interpreted as storehouse for the port. Zarethan, where Solomon cast his bronzes (1 Kings 7:45), may well be the recently excavated Tell es-Saidiyeh, east of the Jordan, since numerous open smelting pits have been found there and suitable ores have been found in the adjacent Arabah valley. It may have been to control this trade that David first subjugated Edom. At Hazor numerous bronze objects, weights, shovels, and a snake emblem for mounting on a pole (like Nehushtan?) have been found. Horned altars of the type used in the temple come from Arad and Beersheba and measure 157 cms (three large royal cubits high) as that of the tabernacle (Exod 27:1) and Solomon's temple (2 Chron 6:13). Supplies for Solomon's kingdom could have come from afar, for he controlled the overland trade routes from Cilicia (Que, so 1 Kings 10:28) to Egypt, and thus the import and export of horses.

Egyptian remains at the Aqabah mines and the destruction of Tel Mor (near Ashdod), Beth-shemesh, and Gezer may be attributed to raids by the Egyptian Siamun early in Solomon's reign. Solomon's ability to contract dynastic marriages with Egyptian and other princesses and to receive Gezer as a marriage gift attests to the power of Israel at that time. The authenticity of an inscribed South Arabian stamp seal from Bethel, dated to the ninth century and formerly thought to confirm Solomon's association with the Queen of Sheba, is now questioned. No native inscriptions of the reign have survived, unless the Gezer calendar (a farmer's almanac or a schoolboy's exercise) is from this reign. The list of Solomon's interests, however, closely parallels the texts studied in both Mesopotamia (HAR-*ra-hubullu*) and Egyptian schools. There, too, wisdom literature and proverbs of all kinds were collected and learned. Lyric poems, like the love songs of the Song of Solomon, survive from Egypt, Syria, and Mesopotamia from the thirteenth century onwards, as do descriptions of a woman by a son to his mother.

4. *The divided kingdom.* Israel was, however, economically

exhausted by the wide-ranging policies undertaken by Solomon and his son Rehoboam, and this was to become a major factor in the defection of the northern kingdom. Rehoboam had to face an invasion by the Libyan usurper who now ruled Egypt. Shishak (Sheshonq I) in his fifth year (c. 928), instigated by the refugee Jeroboam, was only bought off from sacking Jerusalem by being given the temple treasures (1 Kings 14:25, 26). Shishak's triumphal reliefs and text in the Karnak temple of Anun in Thebes show him smiting Asiatic captives and list more than one hundred fifty towns in Phoenicia, Judah, the Esdraelon valley, Edom, and South Syria. A broken stela found at Megiddo attests part of this claim, as do destruction levels at Bethshemesh. Egyptians reinforced the defenses at Sharuhen, and scarabs show their presence also at Gezer, Tell el-'Ajjûl, and Tell Jemmeh. Rehoboam's earlier strengthening of Lachish and Azekah is to be seen in work there.

Jeroboam I had now to find a new center for worship. The part of Bethel (Beitin) thought to be occupied at that time is so far unexcavated. At Dan, where the second golden bull-calf was worshiped as the throne of an invisible god, Biran has unearthed one of the largest city gates yet found in Palestine. He believes the gates were built by Jeroboam. The ferocity of the internal war between Israel and Judah can be seen in Jeroboam's reconstruction work at Shechem and the refortification of Gibeah, of Bethel as the southernmost outpost of the northern capital, and of Tell en-Nasbeh (possibly Mizpah) with its twenty-foot thick walls and towers as the northern outpost of Judah at this time. Such work must have involved conscripted labor (1 Kings 15:15–22). The fortified gateway and courtyard were lined with benches where the elders sat during assemblies, local courts, and major trading transactions.

5. *The dynasty of Omri.* The unsettled northern kingdom found a strong leader in the usurper Omri (884–873 B.C.), who became the sixth king of Israel. The capital at this time was Shechem, where construction work may be assigned to this period (1 Kings 12:25), though it was not a site easily defended. Omri attacked Zimri at Tirzah, seven miles northeast of Shechem and probably to be identified with Tell el Far'ah excavated by de Vaux in 1941–50. The first Iron-Age level there is marked by burning, which may represent Omri's capture of the town, where he lived for six years during the building of his own new capital at Samaria. The site may have been bought so that Omri could be free to organize his own administration on crown property, as David had done at Jerusalem. The incomplete building at Tirzah may be Omri's unfinished palace, and occupation of the area may have continued, according to pottery finds similar to those in early Samaria, until Samaria itself was established when Tirzah was virtually abandoned.

Samaria, excavated carefully and primarily between 1908–1935, shows several occupation levels dating c. 875 –721 B.C. Period I is ascribed to Omri and his son Ahab, who completed his work. The large palace and courtyard on the citadel was surrounded by defenses consisting of three walls, all of fine Phoenician-type bonded masonry. The city gate was approached through a colonnade lined with proto-Ionic (Phoenician) pillars and capitals. These and other finds show that the king was intent on luxury. Doubtless, Ahab was influenced by his alliance with Tyre (1 Kings 16:31), as he was by his wife Jezebel, and doubtless he sought separation from the body of the population. Many ninth- to eighth-century ivory fragments (with Phoenician markings on the reverse) from palace furnishings have been recovered. Ahab's palace could well have earned the reputation of being "a house of ivories" (1 Kings 22:39; Amos 6:4). At the northwest summit a large artificial pool or waterproofed cistern (33 x 17 feet) may well have been the "pool of Samaria" where Ahab's chariot was washed down after his dead body had been carried home in it (1 Kings 22:38).

First Kings 16:21–28 puts most emphasis on the theological appraisal of Omri's life and his failure to put God's law into effective operation ("Omri did evil in the sight of the LORD"), as shown by contemporary Babylonian texts to be the requirement imposed. The Babylonian texts hint at his greatness, and later Assyrian texts refer to Israel at Samaria as "the land or dynasty of Omri." Omri's widespread influence can be judged from the Mesha' stela (The Moabite Stone), found in 1868 and dated c. 830 B.C. On it the king of Moab tells of his father's defeat by Ahab during his thirty-year reign. This was attributed to the anger of the god Chemosh, who, it is said, allowed Omri to occupy the land of Madeba for forty years. The account tells how Moab regained its freedom, probably initially while Ahab was engaged in his war with Syria (2 Kings 1:1) and then finally in the abortive campaign led by Omri's grandson J(eh)oram (2 Kings 3:27). The construction of the Moabite town of *Qrhh* was by Israelite slave-labour. The stela tells how the Israelites had built and occupied the town of Ataroth for the tribe of Gad and Yahaz. It confirms the use of the "ban" (*herem*) and existence of the sanctuaries at high places during this time. Ahab also rebuilt Hazor (Level VIII) and may have been the king responsible for the excavation of the water system of Megiddo.

An Assyrian text of Shalmaneser III tells how he fought a massive battle at Qarqar on the Orontes north of Damascus in 853 B.C. This was against a coalition under

Irhuleni of Hamath and Benhadad II of Aram-Damascus (called Adad-idri or Hadadezer by the Assyrian). This document is the first direct chronological point of reference between Israel and Assyria, for Shalmaneser lists "Ahab the Israelite" as providing "2,000 chariots and 10,000 men." His contribution in chariots was the largest. Musri (Egypt)—together with Cilicia, Arvad, Arabia, and Ammon—provided contingents. The discovery of a presentation vase of Osorkon II in the palace of Samaria may well indicate an Egyptian-Israelite alliance during Ahab's reign. The coalition was effective in halting the Assyrian advance. It is interesting to note the total numbers involved in the Qarqar battle. In addition to their precise numerical use, 10,000 is used to denote an army, 20,000 an army group, 1,000 a battle group, and 100 a company in both Assyrian annals and the OT. Of those who opposed him, Shalmaneser claims to have killed 14,-000 out of the more than 73,000 men, 2,140 chariots, 19,000 cavalry and 1,000 camels.

6. *The last kings of Israel.* By 843 B.C. Hazael had displaced Benhadad II as king of Aram-Damascus and by 841 the usurper Jehu was on the throne of Israel. Hazael, "our lord Haza'el" (*mr'n hz'l*) according to an inscribed ivory fragment found in the plunder from Damascus, now led the Syro-Palestinian nations against Assyria and is so named in a text of Shalmaneser III. The same Assyrian king made Jehu his vassal, according to the Black Obelisk erected in his capital Calah (Nimrud) in 841 B.C. and now in the British Museum. This depicts the bearded "Jehu, son of Omri [i.e., in the ruling line or citizen of Beth Omri] bringing tribute of silver, gold, a gold bowl, a gold vase, gold cups, gold buckets, tin, a staff for the royal hand and . . . fruits." This may well be the only pictorial

representation of any king of Israel to survive, if the kneeling figure who introduces the line of Israelite porters is the king himself and not his representative. This episode is not mentioned in the OT but could show that Jehu sought Assyrian aid against Hazael who was then hostile to Israel (2 Kings 10:32). In this he was unsuccessful, since other Assyrian documents show that Shalmaneser's successor Adad-nirari III, king of Assyria (810–783), was engaged elsewhere and did not venture west until after Jehu's death.

Hazael, "a son of a nobody" (i.e., usurper or illegitimate son) according to the Assyrian annals, attacked and destroyed Megiddo (Level IVA) where the administrative buildings had been rebuilt after Shishak's invasion and a new town (Level III) constructed on the same site but on a different plan. At Samaria (Period III) there was a reconstruction of the palace and fortification by Jehu and his successors when these had been burned down, perhaps by Hazael. The splendor of Omri's Samaria declined, however, and the mediocre buildings (Period III) common to provincial Israel and Judah are now found at that site and elsewhere.

Assyrian attacks on Damascus weakened that kingdom and the pressure on Israel under Joash (801–786) was accordingly relieved (2 Kings 13:24, 25; cf. v.14–19). An Aramaic stela records the triumph of Zakir, king of Hamath and Lu'ash, over Hazael's successor Benhadad III and, though a stone stele of Adad-nirari III from Rimah (west of Mosul) lists Ya'usu (Joash) of Samaria as paying him tribute, together with Mari' of Damascus, there is no evidence that Samaria itself had yet been attacked by the Assyrians. Jeroboam II, the contemporary of Amos (Amos 8:11), appears to have gained great influence during his long and prosperous reign (770–755

B.C.), which coincided with Assyrian weakness. The form
of palace administration already developed by Solomon
continued, so far as can be judged from sixty-three inscribed potsherds from Samaria usually dated to Jeroboam's reign (but to Menahem by others). These record
imports of wine and oil from neighboring crown-estates
and seem to be tax payments made in kind and dated to
regnal years. Yadin thinks these may have been the additional taxes imposed by Menahem to cover the Assyrian
impost of 738. His theory may be supported by the many
biblical names on the ostraca, names that correspond with
the names of Manasseh's descendants (cf. Num 26:29–33;
1 Chron 7:14–19). A large number of Baal names are
included. A seal with the design of a roaring lion and
inscribed "Belonging to Shema', servant of Jeroboam"
shows that this Shema' was a royal official not named in
the OT. That it was Jeroboam II can be judged from the
form of the inscription and its letters.

Azariah (Uzziah) succeeded Jeroboam and seems, at
least initially, to have maintained a wide-ranging influence, since references to *Azriau* of Yaudi (identified with
Judah) in Assyrian texts show him as the active leader of
the anti-Assyria coalition from Judah itself to the Middle
Euphrates.[11] A fine but small royal construction outside
Jerusalem at Ramat Rachel is thought by Aharoni, its
excavator, to be the separate house to which Uzziah was
consigned as a leper later in his reign (2 Kings 15:5).
Similar buildings also made of stone are known from
earlier periods at Samaria and Megiddo. The Aramaic
inscription recording the removal of Uzziah's bones at

---

[11]H. Tadmor, "Azriyau of Yaudi," in *Scripta Hierosolymtana* 8
(1961): 232–271.

Jerusalem is to be dated some seven hundred years after his reign.

Menahem (*menuhimme*) of Samaria is named by Tiglath Pileser, king of Assyria 745–727 B.C., together with sixteen other kings, including Rezin of Damascus, the king mentioned in 2 Kings 15:37; 16:5–9; Isaiah 7:1ff.; 9:11, as bringing tribute to him about 739 B.C. This action may have been inspired by the defeat suffered by Arpad and an attempt to buy time, or by a demand by Assyria for an assurance of goodwill following their conquest of the area north of Damascus. Menahem had to pay one thousand talents of silver by levying fifty shekels from every wealthy Israelite citizen (2 Kings 15:19ff.). This was the equivalent of the value of a slave according to contemporary Assyrian contracts for the sale of slaves and represents a total of 70,000 men. The use of the native name of Pul(u) for Tiglath Pileser in 2 Kings 15:19 is confirmed by the occurrence of this name for him in the Babylonian King List. According to a tablet found at Nimrud (Calah), Tiglath Pileser in 734 attacked the coastal cities of Phoenicia and marched south to Nahalmuṣur ("The River of Egypt"), where he had a stela erected depicting himself as victor. He thus effectively cut off Egypt and Hanun of Gaza, who had fled there, from helping Israel and Judah. Among the towns listed as captured en route was Mahalab (the Meheleb or Ahlab of Judg 1:31) near Sidon.

Two years later the Assyrian relates how he invaded Damascus, which he calls in a broken text "the land of the house of Hazael" (once wrongly read as a reference to the "land of Naphtali") and instigated the murder of Pekah (*Paqaha*), who had foolishly allied himself with Resin of Damascus. He states that he put an Assyrian nominee, Hoshea (*Ausi'*), on the throne of Israel. Towns in the northwest borders of Israel (called "the house of Omri") are named by Tiglath Pileser. They include Abilakku and Gal'za (Galilea or Gilead). Excavations show that the fortified citadel of Hazor was now sacked, though following this campaign the town was the seat of two Assyrian governors, according to texts. In the remains of the city a pot inscribed "Belonging to Pekah" was found. This invasion of Samaria and northern Israel seems to have been in response to the appeal by (Jeho)ahaz of Judah who had refused to join the anti-Assyrian league. According to the Assyrian annals dating from 731 B.C., Jehoahaz (*Yauhazi*) was named with the rulers of Moab, Ashkelon, Edom, and Gaza as paying tribute to Assyria (cf. 2 Kings 16:8). Such aid was given only on condition that the vassal submitted to the treaty terms imposed. These included political and religious supervision, marked by the installation of cult symbols, such as the altar erected by Ahaz in Jerusalem (2 Kings 16:10–16). Despite the warnings of Isaiah (7:9), Ahaz's dependence on Assyria so weakened the state that territory was lost to the coastal city-states and Edom became independent. In this way Judah was cut off from her coastal port of Ezion Geber, which was destroyed by a fierce fire and succeeded by a new Edomite industrial village (Level IV). The unchanged administrative system under Ahaz is perhaps attested by the discovery of a fine carnelian seal inscribed with the name of "Ushnu, official (servant) of Ahaz." A text from Nimrud in Assyria listing tribute from Judah may well date from this reign.

Hoshea of Israel rebelled c. 725, and this brought the inevitable punitive raid predicted in the vassal treaty he had signed with his Assyrian overlord. After Tiglath Pileser's death, his successor Shalmaneser V, according to the Assyrian eponym canon, besieged the city of Samaria for three years (cf. 2 Kings 17:3–6) and the city fell to "the king of Assyria" in 722/1 B.C. The latter could well have been Shalmaneser V himself, as the OT may imply, or his successor as king, Sargon II (722–705 B.C.), who may have taken over in the last stages of the attack or acted jointly with Shalmaneser before his death (note the plural in 2 Kings 18:10). The Babylonian Chronicle records that Shalmaneser "broke [the resistance of] the city of Shama-rain," usually taken to be Samaria rather than the little-known Sibraim (Ezek 47:16). Sargon himself, in annals written in his fourth year at Khorsabad, claims to have been "the conqueror of Samaria," but he does not repeat this in later editions from Nineveh, Calah, or Asshur.

Sargon (who is depicted on his palace wall reliefs at Khorsabad) claims to have taken 27,270 or 27,290 men of Samaria as prisoners. (The number varies according to the date and edition of his annals.) Included in the booty he took were "the gods in whom they trusted," a clear allusion to the polytheism of Israel at this time, though polytheism was so strongly condemned by the prophets. The same text, found at Nimrud in 1952, in words strikingly parallel to Isaiah 13, also describes Sargon's destruction of Babylon. Sargon deported the prisoners from Samaria to Gozan (Guzan, Tell Halaf), where excavation has produced texts bearing names of apparent Jewish exiles. Others were taken to Halah, which, if it is the same as Calah (Nimrud), might account for the list of West Semitic names (Menahem, 'Uzza, Elisha, Hananel, Haza'el, Haggai, etc.) found on an ostracon written by a local scribe. The same Assyrian capital was the place of manufacture of a series of wax-covered ivory and wood writing boards dated 715 B.C. and capable of containing extended literary works equivalent in length to the speeches of Isaiah.

The resettlement of Samaria (now incorporated as an Assyrian province) by groups brought in from Babylonia and elsewhere accords with Sargon's known policy and conquests at this time (2 Kings 17:24). Fragments of pottery from Samaria imply occupation by persons from other parts of Assyria and the ancient Near East.

Hoshea's appeal to Egypt for help against the Assyrians was to "So king of Egypt" (2 Kings 17:4), almost certainly Osorkon IV, the senior pharaoh in the eastern Delta,[12] rather than to an otherwise unknown Egyptian commander, Sib'e, as has been suggested. But no help came from the broken reed of Egypt. By 715–712 it was too late and impossible for help to come, since Sargon marched to Palestine to suppress a revolt by Yamani of Ashdod, where fragments of his victory stela erected there were found in 1963. Destruction levels at Megiddo (III), Hazor, and at Tirzah (II may be 723 B.C.) show the stern action taken. Because the OT is silent as to any incursion into Judah by the Assyrians, it must be assumed that Sargon's claim to be "the subjugator of the land of Judah" (Nimrud building inscription) means that he received tribute from that land. This might have been given when he defeated an alliance of Ashdod and Gath, when they tried to include all Palestine in their antileague, in battle on the Egyptian border near Rapihu in 712. Since the Eponym list states that Sargon himself "stayed in the land" (i.e., Assyria), Isaiah's claim that he sent his commander-in-chief (*turtan*) for these campaigns is correct.

7. *Judah under Assyria.* Judah now had to be prepared to face Assyria alone. On Sargon's death in 705 B.C., Hezekiah decided to break with Assyria, perhaps encouraged

---

[12]K.A. Kitchen, *The Third Intermediate Period in Egypt* (1972), pp. 372–373.

by the action taken by the rebel Marduk-apla-iddina II (Merodach-Baladan) of Babylon whose activities can be followed in Assyrian state records and correspondence. In wise anticipation of the Assyrian reaction, Hezekiah repaired the fortifications of Jerusalem and dug a tunnel to bring water into the city in time of siege (2 Kings 20:20; 2 Chron 32:30). The American explorer Robinson mentions this tunnel in 1838, but it was not cleared until 1880, when an inscription was discovered at the point where the miners working from one end met those excavating from the other 300 feet underneath the surface. Though only six lines remain, this is the second longest monumental text in early Hebrew (now in the Istanbul Museum). It records the work done on this 1,749-foot-long water course:

> ... This is the account of the mining work. While [the men were swinging their] axes, each toward his fellow and while there was still three cubits [4-1/2 feet] to be cut through, the voice of one man calling to the other was heard showing that he was deviating to the right. When the tunnel was driven through, the excavators met man to man, axe against axe, and the water flowed for 1,200 cubits from the spring to the reservoir. The height of the rock above the heads of the excavators was 100 cubits.

In 701 b.c. Sennacherib, son of Sargon and now king of Assyria (705–681 b.c.), sent his army commander (*rab-šarēs*) and chief chamberlain (*rab-šaqeh*) to Jerusalem to parley. There is an interesting parallel to Hezekiah's officials' request that they speak Aramaic rather than the local Hebrew dialect, which would have been readily understood by the bystanders just as it was understood in a letter found at Nimrud. In it the Assyrian generals report their negotiations at Babylon with a Chaldean chief who requested similar action when he opposed entry, despite promises made to the Babylonians as was done to the men of Jerusalem.

Assyrian records provide a commentary on OT history. Sennacherib claims to have "shut up Hezekiah [*Hazaqiau*] the Jew in his royal city Jerusalem like a bird in a cage," but makes no claim to any capture. The Assyrian king himself moved to cut off any possible aid to Jerusalem by defeating the Egyptian army at Eltekeh and by laying siege to Lachish. The dating of these events to a single campaign in 701 B.C. has been questioned, primarily on the assumption that Tirhaka (Taharqa) king of Ethiopia (2 Kings 19:9; Isa 37:9) would have been too young to lead an army. However, revised texts published in 1952 show him to have been about twenty-one in 701 and able to act on behalf of his brother Shebitku. His designation as "king," to which he became entitled as pharaoh of Egypt a few years later, would be in accordance with his responsibilities as ruler of Nubia. The theory that there must have been a conflation of the accounts of two expeditions, the second of which (c. 686) resulted in a defeat for the Assyrians, who omitted it from their records, can no longer be considered likely. The Old Testament account we now have is of one event written from a Judean standpoint.

Hezekiah's tribute of thirty talents of gold is given in both Assyrian and OT sources, but the Assyrians list eight hundred talents of silver as opposed to the three hundred of the Hebrew text. This divergence could be due to a textual corruption in Assyrian or Hebrew records based on a numerical notation, to deviation in the silver measures used, or to different items being included in the reckoning.

Although Sennacherib failed to take Jerusalem, he claims to have laid waste forty-six towns or villages in or surrounding Judah as he did to Lachish (Tell ed-Duweir). Excavations conducted there by J. Starkey for the Wellcome-Marston expedition in 1932–38 show that Level III was destroyed by fire. This is usually attributed to the siege of 701, though others (Albright, Wright, and Kenyon) think it marks the later destruction by the Babylonians in 597 B.C. The walls by the main gate at the southwest show signs of repairs where a breach had been made. In this area were found part of a ramp up which the siege-engines were pushed, and also slingstones, arrowheads, and the crest of a helmet, such as those worn by Assyrian lancers. Since all these are depicted on the bas-reliefs decorating the walls of Sennacherib's (northwest) palace at Nineveh, which bears the caption "Sennacherib, king of Assyria, sitting on his throne while spoil from the city of Lachish passed before him," there can be no question about Lachish having fallen to the Assyrians. A mass grave of more than 1,500 bodies on the northwest slope of the mound and associated with pig bones may show a later (Babylonian?) attempt to desecrate those who had died in the siege. Tell Beit Mirsim, another fortified town in Judah eight miles to the southeast of Lachish, shows partial destruction at this same time.

The Lachish reliefs are important also in that they provide the earliest portrayal of Jewish families being led as prisoners into exile. Barnett has related that, according to the reliefs at Nineveh, some Jews were later shown to be serving in the Assyrian royal bodyguard, and others were shown maneuvering massive stone bull-colossi into position while work was going on at Sennacherib's new palace.

Sennacherib's death as recorded in 2 Kings 19:37

(and Isa 37:38) need not be interpreted as following immediately on his return from Palestine in 701 B.C. The OT says that the murderers were his two sons, Adrammelech (*Arad-malliti*[?]) and Sharezer (*Sar-uṣur*). The Babylonian Chronicle refers to only one son, though other texts tell of family intrigue and the death of an elder brother whom Esarhaddon succeeded as crown-prince, of opposition from his brothers, and of reference by King Ashurbanipal of Assyria thirty-two years later to Sennacherib's murder in a temple at Nineveh.

Esarhaddon of Assyria (681–669) continued to receive tribute from Judah and the Palestinian cities till Tirhaka incited Ba'al of Tyre to rebel. The Assyrian annals detail Esarhaddon's success in Egypt and list his vassals, who included "Manasseh (Minse), King of Judah" between Ba'al of Tyre and Qaush(Chemosh)-gabri of Edom. The kings of Moab, Gaza, Ashkelon, Ekron, Gebal, Arvad, Ashdod, and Beth-Ammon are also named by the Assyrian king. It may be that an undated Assyrian text listing payments belongs to this time. Ammon contributed two minas of gold, Moab one mina, and Judah, as probably Edom also, sent two minas of silver.

In May 672 B.C. Esarhaddon summoned Manasseh and his other vassals to Calah where he imposed on them new obligations to ensure continued loyalty to Assyria and to his successors. The texts containing the "covenant" requirements have survived and show the unchanged legal form known from the second millennium B.C. (see D.2 above). These required the vassals to take the god of Assyria as their god and threatened destruction of their cities and exiles for their citizens, should they break any of the terms.

The fiscal organization of Judah can be followed in the taxes paid in kind to the king (*lmlk*) in jars with stamped handles showing the collection centers—Hebron, Sokoh, Ziph, and *mmšt*—and bearing a symbol of a four-winged scarab-beetle for the reign of Hezekiah, a more stylized form with inscription in a later style for the reign of Manasseh, and a winged flying scroll for the period of Josiah and his successors (640–587 B.C.). About six hundred of these jar handles are known, a large number coming from Tell en-Nasbeh(Mizpah) and Lachish.

The aging Ashurbanipal handed over power or died in c. 627 B.C. and the outlying vassal states, including Babylonia and Judah, soon rebelled. Josiah proclaimed his independence from Assyrian domination by instigating religious and social reforms. In 609 he lost his life attacking Megiddo, once an Assyrian fortified outpost but by now taken over by the Egyptians (2 Kings 23:29). His hostility to the Egyptians, whom he sought to prevent from going to reinforce the beleaguered Assyrian government at Harran (to which it had withdrawn on the fall of Nineveh to the Medes in 612), can be seen in the destruction level (II) there. Megiddo ceased thereafter to be of major importance. The expedition by Necho II of Egypt to aid the Assyrians is recounted in the Babylonian Chronicle, which proves to be an objective, reliable, and unique historical source for many events between 626 and 595, and between 556 and 539 B.C.

8. *The Babylonian domination.* The same Chronicle describes the Babylonian attacks against towns in the Middle Euphrates area that culminated in the sack of Carchemish in the early summer of 605 B.C. Excavations there show that there was fierce fighting within the city, which was stubbornly defended until it was ravaged by fire. Objects found there show that the Egyptian garrison included Greek mercenaries. The Chronicle says that the survivors

fled to Hamath, which was taken by the Babylonians. In the following years (604–603 B.C.), the Babylonians marched unopposed through Palestine ("Hatti-land"). Heavy tribute was brought to them by all the kings and with it many prisoners (including Daniel) were sent back to Babylon. Jehoiakim of Judah, who was to be a faithful vassal for three years, no doubt submitted during these incursions. The primary named target of these Babylonian campaigns was Ashkelon, which was sacked, and this led to the fast proclaimed by Jeremiah (36:1–9). An Aramaic letter from a Palestinian ruler to a king of Egypt appealing for help against the king of Babylon, whose army had advanced as far as Aphek (Ras el 'Ain, northeast of Joppa), may be connected with this event. Others, however, argue that the letter was a request for aid by Gaza or Ashdod when Nebuchadnezzar attacked in 589–587. This papyrus letter from Saqqara incidentally shows that Aramaic was the international diplomatic language of the day. According to the Chronicle, in 601 B.C. the Babylonians met the Egyptians in a fierce clash that resulted in such heavy casualties that the Babylonians spent the next year re-equipping. This would explain the swing in Jehoiakim's allegiance to Egypt despite Jeremiah's warnings (Jer 27:9–11). Pressure was gradually brought to bear on Judah and her neighbors, especially the Arabian tribes whose deities had been taken from them. The anxiety of the time is reflected by Jeremiah (49:28–33). The Babylonian Chronicle continues:

> In his [Nebuchadnezzar's] seventh year he called up his army and marched to Palestine. He besieged the city of Judah [i.e., Jerusalem], and on the second day of the month of Adar he siezed the city and captured its king. He appointed there a king of his own choice,

received its heavy tribute, and sent [them] off to Babylon. (Cf. 2 Kings 24:10–17.)

This external evidence for the first capture of Jerusalem, now dated to 16 March, 597 B.C., is of primary importance. It provides a further firm point in both biblical and
Babylonian chronology for this event and for the beginning of the exile. The captured king is the young Jehoiachin, who three months earlier had succeeded the dead
Jehoiakim. He is named (*Yaukin*) in economic texts from
Babylon dated between 595–570 B.C. These texts detail
the issue of rations of oil and barley from the royal stores
in Babylon. They also name eight other Judeans together
with other royalty and craftsmen from Egypt, Philistia
(Ashkelon), Phoenicia, Syria, Cilicia, Lydia, Elam, Media,
and Persia who were held in Babylon. Some of these
places are the specific objects of prophecy in Jeremiah.
Jehoiachin, though a hostage, is still called "King of
Judah"; his estates there continued to be managed till 587
B.C. by "Eliakim, steward of Jehoiachin." Impressions of
Eliakim's seal were found at Debir and Beth Shemesh.

The king chosen by Nebuchadnezzar as substitute for
Jehoiachin was his uncle Mattaniah-Zedekiah (2 Kings
24:17). The heavy tribute included the sacred temple vessels that were dispatched to Babylon "at the turn of the
year" (i.e., May/June, 2 Chron 36:10) with the captives.

The last days of Judah are also graphically illustrated
by inscribed ostraca from Lachish. Most are written by
Hoshaiah, a watchpost commander near Azekah north of
Lachish, to Yaosh the commander of that city. They reflect the state of the country as it awaited the advance of
the Babylonian army in 589–587, or soon thereafter to
avenge Zedekiah's defection and reliance on Egypt. Communication between the forts was by fire signal (Jer 6:1;

34:7). The end of Judah as a state is marked by the large number of towns destroyed at this time and never occupied again: Lachish, Azekah (2 Kings 24:7), Tell Beit Mirsim, Beth Shemesh (II), and Ramat Rachel. Although there is little direct archaeological evidence for the destruction of Jerusalem in 587, there can be no question that the city was so severely raped that it would be difficult to trace the material remains of the humble existence endured by the survivors. Vincent attributes the mass grave in the Kidron valley to this destruction. The end of Tell Arad (Level VI) seems to indicate the deliberate policy of eliminating all the Iron Age III rectangular fortresses along the southern frontier, including Kadesh-Barnea.

9. *The period of the Exile.* If Tell en-Nasbeh in Palestine, rather than Nebi Samwil, is to be identified with Mizpah, then its continued occupation after the fall of Jerusalem shows it to have been the new capital of Judah and the center of the administration. Jar handles and containers for tax payments do still have "Judah" (*yhd*) or, more rarely, "Jerusalem" inscribed on them, and a few bear personal names. The majority are inscribed "Mizpah" (*msp*) and those with *msh*, if not also a reference to Mizpah, which continued an important center into the late Persian period, are to Mosah (cf. Josh 21:26), northwest of Jerusalem. Gezer also seems to have remained of importance until c. 100 B.C., and a Babylonian tablet has been found there. A clay sealing with the name of the pro-Babylonian governor—"Belonging to Gedaliah who is over the house"—was found at Lachish. This implies that at this time that city fell within Gedaliah's jurisdiction (Jer 34:7; 40:5). The presence at Mizpah of a bronze circlet inscribed "king of the world" in cuneiform, dated between

800 and 650 B.C., might imply that Nebuchadnezzar went there on his way to Egypt. Other objects from the site include a fine seal with the representation of a fighting cock inscribed "Belonging to Jaazaniah, the minister [servant] of the king"; perhaps he was one of the persons who murdered Gedaliah at Mizpah (2 Kings 25:23–25; Jer 40:8). In contrast, the towns of Megiddo, Bethel, and Samaria in the northern Assyrian province were left untouched, though probably occupied by garrisons since objects of the late Babylonian period have been found there.

In Babylonia itself in the time of the exile the splendor of Nebuchadnezzar's capital can be reconstructed from the results of the German excavations there. The northern citadel incorporated a museum, the southern was entered by the Ishtar Gate, one of eight named city gates. It incorporated a royal palace with a large throne room that might have been the one later used by Belshazzar, and the storeroom in which the ration tablets naming Jehoiachin were discovered. A sacred procession way ran from the Ishtar Gate for almost a mile to Esagila, the temple of Marduk, and its seven-staged temple tower (ziggurat). This road, named "The Enemy Shall Not Prevail," was forty feet wide and led to a bridge with seven piers that spanned the River Euphrates to give access to the new city. Texts list more than fifty temples in this city of which Nebuchadnezzar was so proud (Dan 4:30). Fifteen of these had been built by the king himself and the city was conspicuous for its many statues (Jer 50:38). There were 180 open-air shrines dedicated to the goddess Ishtar alone. The massive defense walls and flood defenses were to prove useless. Cyrus captured the city without a battle. The Persian army gained entry by diverting the river upstream at Opis and then marching down the dried-up riverbed under the walls. The Babylonian Chronicle records this strategy and the fall of Babylon, which occurred in October 539 B.C. It tells also of the disappearance of the Babylonian king Nabonidus, whose son Belshazzar, named in a Babylonian royal inscription as coregent, had acted as king for ten years while his father was absent in Tema' in central Arabia at a Babylonian-Jewish colony centered in Yathrib (Medina). This might in some way reflect the exile of the mad Nabonidus, who, like Nebuchadnezzar, was called Labynetus by Herodotus (I.188). Nabonidus, according to his Harran inscription, had returned to Babylon c. 546 on receiving assurances from the king of Egypt and the "king of the Medes," who at this time must have been Cyrus. This writer has suggested that since there is no record in any Babylonian historical text of any king ruling between Nabonidus/Belshazzar and Cyrus, or Cyrus and Cambyses, "Darius the Mede" may be a throne-name for Cyrus. Thus Daniel 6:28 could be translated "Daniel prospered in the reign of Darius even [i.e.,] the reign of Cyrus the Persian."[13] Whitcomb, however, rejects this, identifying Darius with the little-known Gubaru/Gobryas, a provincial governor of Babylon and Transpotamia.[14]

Cyrus in a Persian Verse Account shows his hostility to the defeated Nabonidus. In another document he records his proclamation by which he sent back from Babylon to their respective temples all the gods that had been brought to Babylon. This edict included the Jews who, having no gods to take back, were given a contribution toward the rebuilding of their temple (cf. Ezra 1:2–4).

---

[13]D.J. Wiseman, *Notes on Some Problems of the Book of Daniel* (London: Inter-Varsity Press, 1965).

[14]J.C. Whitcomb, *Darius the Mede*, Grand Rapids: Eerdmans, 1959.

Thus, the arrival of the Persians in Babylon seems to have been peaceful and resulted in few innovations.

The return of the Jews to Judah can be seen in the sparse traces of resettlement found at Gezer, Lachish, Bethel, Beth-zur (north of Hebron), and Tell el-Far'ah. It was a slow process, and the country does not seem to have recovered until the third century B.C. The Phoenicians—to judge by settlements at Athlit, Dor, the site of the later Caesarea, and near Jaffa—seized the chance to expand their territory. Elsewhere (e.g., Tel Abu Hawam) the houses show a clear continuation in style from the early Iron Age.

Judah now formed part of the fifth satrapy of the Persian (Achaemenid) empire called "Beyond the River." This meant that it was dominated by the subgovernor at Samaria, who worked under the direction of Damascus. Sanballat (*Sin-uballit*) is named in papyri from Elephantine (Yeb), which include letters to his sons as well as to Johanan the high-priest of the Jerusalem temple (Neh 12:22, 23). The same group of exiles appealed in 407 B.C. to Bagoas, governor of Arabia, to whom is attributed the fine villa at Lachish with its distinctive columned and vaulted rooms (perhaps a Persian or Babylonian innovation). This building was protected by walls rebuilt by the fifth century on top of those destroyed by Nebuchadnezzar. Geshem is named in an inscription from Hegra in Arabia and on a silver vessel from Tell el Maskuteh (Succoth) in Egypt inscribed in Aramaic "Qainu, son of Geshem, King of Kedar." The third adversary named by Nehemiah (6:1), Tobiah of Ammon, the founder of the ruling dynasty in Jordan, may well be the ancestor of the Ammonite Tobiah who sent a letter to Zeno, an official of Ptolemy Philadelphus (285–246 B.C.) and of the Tobiah whose name is inscribed in a rock-hewn tomb at 'Araq el-Emir in Jordan built by the last governor in the family c. 200–175 B.C.

Texts from the reign of Darius I dated between 21 March, 520, and 31 October, 519 B.C., show that Ushtannu (the Hystanes of Herodotus VII,177) was "Governor of Babylon and Beyond the River [*Eber nāri*]" and subordinate to him as the local governor of "Beyond the River" was one Tattanu (Tattenai of Ezra 5:3, 6; 6:6, 13) according to his own texts, one of them dating to 5 June, 502 B.C.[15]

The economy of the period of the exile can be judged from the many economic and administrative texts from Babylonia for which the cuneiform script was still used. Many Hebrew (and Aramaic) personal names are found in transactions sponsored by the Egibi family and by the house of Murashu and sons, whose records span several decades and show a vigorous community. Judah was allowed to strike its own coinage, inscribed *Yhd* (once mistakenly read as *Yh*=Yahweh).

10. *The Hellenistic age.* (331–63 B.C.). When Alexander took over the Persian empire in 333, Hellenization grew apace. From his death (323) to c. 198, Palestine was controlled by the Ptolemies (Lagides) of Egypt and lay on their frontier with the Seleucids in Syria. Trade with Greece had begun earlier and its development had been encouraged by mercenaries who followed earlier intruders like Necho and Nebuchadnezzar and by the local autonomy allowed under Persian rule. The progress can be seen in the imports of Greek Ionian and Attic black-figured and other wares from the sixth century onwards

[15]A.F. Rainey, "The Satrapy 'Beyond the River,'" in *Australian Journal of Biblical Archaeology* I, 1969, p.53.

at coastal ports, including the Greek fort at Ashdod and at Hazor(I) and by the introduction of coinage when imitations of Attic coins were minted in the late fifth century. Similar numismatic influences from Arabia are found in the south.

Lachish was deserted and the newly planned Greek city of Marisa shows a combination of Greek, Phoenician, and Edomite influences, painted tombs, and pottery. Ptolemy II rebuilt Amman (Philadelphia) and Jarash (Antioch), but Nabatean culture thrived alongside these Hellenistic strongholds.

The Seleucid period has left the mausoleum of the Tobiad family at ‘Araq el-Emir in early Hellenistic style with Corinthian capitals. At Samaria the old Israelite walls were strengthened by a series of Hellenistic round towers (c. 323–1). This was superseded by a fortress with four-meter-thick walls as part of the defenses in the war between the Seleucids and the Maccabees. The presence of a Greek garrison is inferred from the 2,000 or more Rhodian wine-jar handles found here and by ostraca at Arad. Shechem, rebuilt between 330–100 B.C., also appears to have been occupied by a Greek garrison, perhaps there to control a resurgent Samaritan religious community. The town was destroyed by John Hyrcanus in 107 B.C., by which time coins on the site cease. Beth-zur, on the boundary with Idumea, had an extensive Hellenistic-type citadel-fortress, rebuilt by Judas Maccabeus on the site used by the Macedonian general Bacchides for his fortifications (c. 161 B.C., 1 Macc 9:52). Coins date the periods of occupation to the time of Antiochus IV (Epiphanes, 175–164 B.C.) and his son Antiochus Eupator (164 –162). The attempt of Antiochus Epiphanes to suppress Judaism and its temple led to the Maccabean revolt. Houses, shops, and water cisterns show a lively economy;

and the jar handles inscribed with the name of the potter, magistrate, or tax collector over a number of years attest the presence of a Greek garrison and the maintenance of order. Gezer was fortified by the Maccabees c. 140, and outside the town an inscription in the rocks marks the boundary of a sabbath day's walk. Gezer, like Beth-zur and Marisa, was abandoned c. 100 B.C., probably when Alexander Janneus removed the garrison when Palestine was under his firm and peaceful rule. At this time Qumrān was occupied and the pre-Herodian buildings and cisterns at Masada were also his work. By 37 B.C. the Herodian dynasty replaced the Maccabees, and under Herod the Great Hellenistic architecture and culture flourished.

Bibliography

Books

Albright, W.F. *The Archaeology of Palestine.* Harmondsworth: Penguin Books, 1960.

Anati, E. *Palestine Before the Hebrews.* London: Jonathan Cape, 1963.

Burrows, M. *What Mean These Stones?* London: Thames and Hudson, 1957.

Franken, H.J. and Franken-Battershill, C.A. *A Primer of Old Testament Archaeology.* Leiden: Brill, 1963.

Freedman, D.N. and Wright, G.E. *The Biblical Archaeologist Reader* I. Garden City, New York: Doubleday, 1969.

Harding, G.L. *The Antiquities of Jordan.* London: Lutterworth, 1959.

Kenyon, K.M. *Archaeology in the Holy Land.* London: Ernest Benn, 1960.

Kitchen, K.A. *Ancient Orient and Old Testament.* London: Tyndale, 1966.

Oppenheim, A.L. *Ancient Mesopotamia.* Chicago: University of Chicago Press, 1964.

Sanders, J.A. *Near Eastern Archaeology in the Twentieth Century.* Garden City, New York: Doubleday, 1970.

Thomas, D.W., ed. *Archaeology and Old Testament Study.* London: Oxford University Press, 1967.

Unger, M.F. *Archaeology and the Old Testament.* Grand Rapids: Zondervan, 1962.

Wiseman, D.J. *Chronicles of Chaldaean Kings (626–556 B.C.) in the British Museum.* London: British Museum, 1956.

_____, ed. *Peoples of Old Testament Times.* Oxford: Clarendon, 1973.

Wright, G.E. "The Archaeology of Palestine." In *The Bible and the Ancient Near East,* edited by G.E. Wright. London: Routledge and Kegan Paul, 1961.

_____. *Biblical Archaeology.* Philadelphia: Westminster, 1962.

Yamauchi, E. *The Stones and the Scriptures.* London: Inter-Varsity, 1973; Philadelphia and New York: Lippincott, 1972.

Periodicals

The Biblical Archaeologist (American School for Oriental Research)

Israel Exploration Journal (Jerusalem)

Levant (London: British School of Archaeology in Jerusalem)

Palestine Exploration Quarterly (London: Palestine Exploration Fund).

ARCHAEOLOGY AND THE
NEW TESTAMENT

Preface to
Archaeology and the New Testament

Archaeological discoveries in the eastern Mediterranean area—particularly texts in Hebrew, Aramaic, Greek, and Latin—have helped us to recreate the world of the New Testament. These finds help us to understand the background of Jesus' parables, to visualize the cities of Paul, and to understand the allusions of the Apocalypse.

For those who are fortunate enough to visit the Holy Land and to follow the footsteps of Paul, a knowledge of New Testament archaeology will enable such modern pilgrims to discern between probably authentic sites and those of late or dubious attestation. Much of the information provided by tourist guides is to be taken with a grain of skepticism. Yet radiocarbon tests have recently shown that some of the olive trees in the Garden of Gethsemane may go back to the time of Jesus after all.

In some cases, as in Old Testament archaeology, excavations have provided direct evidence to temper the hyper-skepticism of some biblical critics. In most examples, the major contribution of archaeology has been to make vivid the setting of the New Testament—to remind us that our Lord and His followers were flesh-and-blood persons who trod the dusty paths of Palestine and the paved roads of the Roman Empire.

The discovery a young man's heel bones still transfixed by an iron nail brings home to us the harsh reality of the Crucifixion. Actual graves with rolling stones enable us to picture the empty tomb of Christ, though only faith in the Risen Lord can make clear the latter's significance.

Edwin Yamauchi

ARCHAEOLOGY AND THE NEW TESTAMENT

Introduction

Ramsay and the Tübingen School

The radical skepticism of F.C. Baur and his Tübingen school of criticism was tempered by the development of NT archaeology in the late nineteenth and early twentieth centuries.

W.F. Albright rendered this verdict on radical NT criticism:

In the same way, the form-critical school founded by M. Dibelius and R. Bultmann a generation before the discovery of the Dead Sea Scrolls has continued to flourish without the slightest regard for the Dead Sea Scrolls. In other words, all radical schools in New Testament criticism which have existed in the past or which exist today are prearchaeological, and are, therefore, since they were built *in der Luft* ["in the air"], quite antiquated today.[1]

The first to see that the archaeological data did not fit the theories of scholars but rather confirmed the NT itself, especially the writings of Luke, was the great archaeologist of Asia Minor, Sir William Ramsay.[2] When he began his researches at the end of the nineteenth century, he had accepted the views of the Tübingen school about the late date and unreliability of Acts. The results of his own discoveries convinced him of the essential trustworthiness of the NT.[3] His researches and conclusions influenced scholars such as T. Zahn, A. Harnack, E. Meyers, and A.T. Olmstead to view the NT in a positive light. Ramsay's work has continued to influence such British NT scholars as F.F. Bruce and such classical historians as A.N. Sherwin-White.[4]

On the other hand, German commentators on Acts have virtually ignored the archaeological researches of

---

[1]W.F. Albright in *The Teacher's Yoke*, ed. E.J. Vardaman (Waco: Baylor University Press, 1964), p. 29.

[2]W.W. Gasque, *Sir William M. Ramsay* (Grand Rapids: Baker, 1966).

[3]W.M. Ramsay, *The Bearing of Recent Discovery on the Trustworthiness of the New Testament* (Grand Rapids: Baker, 1953 repr. of the 1915 ed.); C.J. Hemer, *Tyndale Bulletin* 22 (1971): 119–124; idem, BJRL 60 (1977): 28–51.

[4]Cf. E. Yamauchi, *The Stones and the Scriptures* (Philadelphia: Lippincott, 1972), pp. 96–98.

Ramsay and have interpreted Luke's work primarily from a literary-theological perspective. Gasque explains the reason for the difference in approaches as follows:

> An important feature of early British criticism is that it was rooted firmly in historical study. Those who became the leading New Testament critics had received their preparation for this task by a careful and minute study of the classics and ancient history. This underlined for them the importance of the true environment of the New Testament writings, *viz.* The Hellenic world at large. It also prepared them to recognize the important contribution of archaeological research to the study of the New Testament as soon as this new science appeared on the scene.
>
> In contrast to criticism in Germany, British biblical scholarship was never the handmaid of philosophy.[5]

Monuments, Materials, and Texts

NT archaeology encompasses the areas of the eastern Mediterranean, following the course of the spread of the gospel as it radiated from the Holy Land especially through the missionary endeavors of Paul. The areas therefore of the greatest interest are, first of all, Palestine, Jordan, and Syria;[6] then Anatolia (Turkey), Greece, and Italy.[7]

In these areas many monuments have always remained visible, such as the temple platform in Jerusalem,

---

[5]W.W. Gasque, *A History of the Criticism of the Acts of the Apostles* (Grand Rapids: Eerdmans, 1975), p. 108; idem, *Theologische Zeitschrift* 28 (1972): 177–96. Cf. F.F. Bruce, NTS 22 (1976): 229–42.

[6]M. Avi-Yonah, *The Holy Land* (Grand Rapids: Baker, 1966); E. Yamauchi, JAAR 42 (1974): 710–26.

[7]C.F. Pfeiffer and H.F. Vos, *The Wycliffe Historical Geography of Bible Lands* (Chicago: Moody, 1968).

the Parthenon in Athens, and the Colosseum in Rome. The vast bulk of monuments, inscriptions, and material remains have been recovered, however, in the course of archaeological excavations.

Archaeologists have uncovered remains of buildings, streets, siege works, mosaics, furniture, tombs, pottery, etc. In some cases these discoveries can be correlated with the NT or with Josephus, the Jewish historian who wrote at the end of the first century A.D.

Inscribed texts primarily in Hebrew, Aramaic, Greek, and Latin are of utmost interest for our understanding of the NT. The most sensational finds in this regard are the famed Dead Sea Scrolls from Qumran.

The great mass of Greek inscriptions relating to the Jews are brief funerary inscriptions such as those found on ossuaries—limestone boxes for the redeposit of the bones of the dead. Of 683 published Jewish Greek inscriptions from the Diaspora, 65 are from a cemetery in Cyrenaica, 80 from Tell el-Yehudieh in Egypt, and 262 from catacombs in Rome.[8] The dominant position of Greek among the Jews of the Diaspora may be seen from a study of catacomb inscriptions from Rome, which shows that 74 percent were in Greek, 24 percent in Latin, and only 2 percent in Hebrew or Aramaic.[9]

Of the greatest value for dating purposes are coins, which are primarily of bronze but occasionally of silver. The coins of the various Herodian rulers and Roman procurators are quite revealing. Herod the Great's coins were mainly aniconic (without images) but in later years

---

[8]G. Mussies in *The Jewish People in the First Century*, ed. S. Safrai and M. Stern (Philadelphia: Fortress, 1974), 1042–43.
[9]H.J. Leon, *The Jews of Rome* (Philadelphia: Jewish Publication Society, 1960).

he introduced the eagle, symbol of Roman might. Herod Philip, who ruled in a largely Gentile region in the northeast, decorated his coins with the images of the emperor and of the god Pan (cf. Panias or Caesarea Philippi, which he founded). The Jewish zealots superimposed their own inscriptions on Roman coins, proudly proclaiming their mottos of independence.[10]

The coin most often mentioned in the NT is the silver denarius or "penny," which was the equivalent of a day's wage. The coin with Caesar's image shown to Jesus (Matt 22:19–21) probably bore the likeness of either Tiberius or Augustus. Other coins such as those mentioned in Luke 15: 8–9 were Tyrian shekels of silver, which were considered acceptable for the temple offering.[11]

Archaeology and the New Testament Periods

Herod the Great

When Jesus was born in Bethlehem, the king of Judaea was Herod the Great (37–4 B.C.). None of his coins bears his image. But at Seeia in the Hauran in Jordan there once stood a statue of Herod, of which only the base remains. H. Ingholt has suggested that a colossal head from Egypt acquired by the Boston Museum may well depict Herod.[12]

Herod was highly regarded by the Romans as a loyal client king and able military leader. An Athenian inscription calls him *philorōmaios*, "friend of the Romans." According to Josephus, Herod used his vast wealth in

---

[10]Y. Meshorer, *Jewish Coins* (Tel Aviv: Am Hassefer, 1967).

[11]A. Spijkerman, *Liber Annuus* 6 (1955–56): 279–98.

[12]*Journal of the American Research Center in Egypt* 2 (1964): 125–42.

benefactions to many foreign cities and even provided funds for the Olympic Games.

Herod was the most prodigious builder in Israel since the days of Solomon. The beautiful buildings that adorned Jerusalem in the days of Jesus were erected by him.

1. *Jerusalem.* Herod's greatest undertaking was the complete rebuilding of the second temple of Zerubbabel. The rabbis said, "Whoever has not seen Herod's temple has never seen a beautiful building." Nearly twenty thousand workmen, including one thousand priests, labored on the task. Work was begun in the eighteenth year of Herod's reign, and the essential structures, including the massive platform, were completed by 9 B.C. Additional work continued, however, until about A.D. 64, only six years before the Romans razed the temple. When Jesus was challenged by his opponents, "It has taken forty-six years to build this temple, and you are going to raise it in three days?" (John 2:20), the date must have been about A.D. 27/28.

The excavations made by B. Mazar (1968–77) have brought into view additional courses of the finely drafted stones of the southwest section of the Herodian platform. These stones elicited the admiring comment of the disciples, "Look Teacher! What massive stones! What magnificent buildings!" (Mark 13:1). The limestone ashlars (hewn stones) average 3 to 4 feet in height and in some cases are almost 40 feet long. The larger stones weigh more than 100 tons.

At the southwest corner of the platform the springing of an arch, first identified by Robinson in the nineteenth century, has long been visible. In 1968 Mazar uncovered the lower pier of the arch. We now understand that the arch supported not a viaduct but a monumental staircase used by Herod and his family.

Wilson's Arch to the north is 10 feet below the modern street in front of the Gate of the Chain. It once supported a viaduct used by the priests to gain access to the temple.

A paved road ran along the western wall (the "Wailing Wall") and extended nearly a mile south. Under this street a water conduit led in the same direction.

The main entrances for the people were the two Huldah Gates on the southern side of the platform. The eastern gate is now a blocked triple gate; the blocked western gate is partially visible under the Al-Aksah Mosque. A recent examination of the interior shows that 85 percent of its construction goes back to the NT period. Jesus and his disciples must have entered by the eastern gate and exited by the western gate.

Before the western gate, Mazar uncovered a monumental stairway with thirty steps, over 200 feet wide. He also discovered the tunnels, called *mesibot*, designed for the quick exit of people and objects that had become defiled.

In the eastern section of the platform was the Susa Gate, probably where the Golden Gate is located today. The latter was blocked up by a Muslim ruler in 1530 to frustrate the prophecy of Ezekiel 44:1–2.[13] In 1969 an earlier gate, which may possibly have been the Herodian gate through which Jesus passed on Palm Sunday, was sighted about 8 feet below the bottom of the present Golden Gate.[14]

Above the southern edge of the platform was built the

---

[13]S. Steckoll, *The Gates of Jerusalem* (Tel Aviv: Am Hassefer, 1968), pp. 13–14.

[14]G. Giacumakis, *The Bulletin of the Near East Archaeological Society* 4 (1974): 23–26.

magnificent Royal Portico, a triple colonnade 800 feet long. Mazar found a block from the parapet of the southwestern corner with a Hebrew inscription, *le-beit hat-teqi'ah* "for the place of the blowing' [of the trumpet]," which refers to the blowing of the ram's horn to announce the beginning and the end of the Sabbath. Other interesting objects found in the area include a fragment of a sundial, a limestone object inscribed *qorban* ("offering"; Mark 7:11), and Corinthian capitals of columns with gilded leaves.

The area on the platform was divided into a court open to the Gentiles and the smaller area around the temple proper. On a stone balustrade around this inner area warnings in Greek and in Latin were placed. In 1871 a Greek copy of the warning inscription was found; in 1935 a fragmentary Greek copy was found near St. Stephen's Gate. The text reads: "Let no Gentile enter within the balustrade and enclosure about the holy place; and whosoever is caught shall be responsible to himself because death follows."[15]

When Paul returned to Jerusalem for the last time, he precipitated a riot because the Jews believed that he had taken a Gentile into the inner area of the temple (Acts 21:27–30). Paul was no doubt referring to this barrier when he wrote of the middle wall of partition between Jew and Gentile—the wall that had been broken down by Christ (Eph 2:14).

The gate separating the Court of the Women from the Court of Israel to the west was the ornate gate donated by Nicanor, a wealthy Alexandrian. At the beginning of this century an ossuary was discovered on Mount Scopus,

---

[15]J.H. Iliffe, *Quarterly of the Department of Antiquities in Palestine* 6 (1938): 1–3.

bearing the name of Nicanor the Alexandrian. More recently an ossuary from Giv'at ha-Mivtar, Jerusalem, which bore the Aramaic inscription "Simon, builder of the temple," was recovered.

A. Muehsam has attempted a reconstruction of the facade of the temple building itself from the design on the coins of Bar Kochba.[16] M. Avi-Yonah has constructed this design on a model of Jerusalem in the scale of 1:50 on the grounds of the Holy Land Hotel in Jerusalem.[17]

In the Citadel area (Jaffa Gate) Herod had erected three great towers named Hippicus, Phasael, and Mariamne. Above the bases were added superstructures, including cisterns and living quarters, which made the towers about 100 feet high. The present "David's Tower" is built on the base of Phasael.

In the area south of the Citadel and extending to the Armenian Gardens, R. Amiran and A. Eitan have uncovered the foundations of Herod's palace over 1,000 feet long and 200 feet broad. Only a few rooms in the northwest corner have been preserved.[18] In 1977 M. Broshi uncovered sections of Herod's city wall near the Citadel.

2. *Sebaste.* Herod in 26 B.C. rebuilt the city of Samaria and renamed it *Sebaste* (the Greek equivalent of Augustus) in honor of the emperor. Herod settled six thousand of his veterans here. On the acropolis the broad staircase of the temple dedicated to Augustus survives; nearby the torso of a white marble statue of the emperor was discovered.

---

[16]A. Muehsam, *Coin and Temple* (Leeds: Leeds University Press, 1966).

[17]M. Avi-Yonah in *Studies in the History of Religions XIV*, ed. J. Neusner (Leiden: Brill, 1968), pp. 327–35.

[18]R. Amiran and A. Eitan, *Israel Exploration Journal* 22 (1972): 50–51.

One may also see the remains of the basilica, the great public building of the forum. On the plains below are the remains of a stadium that may possibly be Herodian in date. The theater and the colonnaded street are from later constructions of the second and third centuries.

3. *Caesarea.* One of the most significant projects of Herod was his construction of the artificial harbor at Caesarea, begun in 22 B.C. and dedicated to Augustus in 10 B.C. The enormous stone blocks, 50 by 18 feet, that Herod used to build the protective moles of the harbor have been located. In 1960 an underwater expedition recovered a coin that depicts the entrance to the harbor.[19]

Within the area of the Crusader city of Caesarea may be seen the podium of a building that has been identified as the temple dedicated to Augustus. Fragments of colossal statues, probably of Augustus and of Rome personified, have been recovered.

The city was supplied with water by two aqueducts: a low-level aqueduct 3 miles long and a high-level aqueduct 6 miles long.[20] The latter was built by Herod. Numerous Latin inscriptions of soldiers of the VIth, Xth, and XIIth legions record repairs made in Hadrian's reign. It has been suggested that one of the soldiers mentioned in an inscription may have been a son of the historian Josephus.[21]

From 1959 to 1961 an Italian expedition excavated the 4,500-seat theater. The theater may have been the scene of Herod Agrippa I's fatal stroke (Acts 12:21–23). R. Bull, on the other hand, favors the site of the amphi-

---

[19]C.T. Fritsch, BA 24 (1961): 50–59.
[20]Y. Olam and Y. Peleg, *Israel Exploration Journal* 27 (1977): 127–37.
[21]L.I. Levine, *Caesarea Under Roman Rule* (Leiden: Brill, 1975), p. 37.

theater, which appears to have been larger than the Colosseum in Rome. Soundings have been made in the second-century A.D. hippodrome, which was used for chariot races.

In one of the extensive warehouses on the sea front, R. Bull discovered in 1973 a third- or fourth-century A.D. mithraeum, which is the first ever to be discovered in Israel.[22]

4. *Jericho.* Herodian Jericho is located along both banks of the Wadi Qelt to the south of OT Jericho. Excavations by J.L. Kelso in 1950 and by J.B. Pritchard in 1951 have discovered some of the splendid buildings erected by Herod south of the wadi. They uncovered a great sunken garden, 360 feet long, adorned with statuary niches and flower pots. The use of concrete and special masonry reflects the use of Roman craftsmen.

Recent excavations by E. Netzer have uncovered a palatial area north of the wadi. The most interesting discovery was a swimming pool, 100 by 60 feet—no doubt the pool in which Herod had the high priest Aristobulus III drowned (Jos. Antiq. XV, 53–56).[23]

5. *Masada.* The most spectacular site in Israel is Masada, the plateau shaped like a battleship and located on the western shore of the Dead Sea. The site, developed by Herod between 37 and 31 B.C., became the last stronghold of the Jews against the Romans in A.D. 73 (see below under *The Jewish Revolt*, pp. 104–7). Excavations from 1963 to

---

[22]R. Bull, *Israel Exploration Journal* 24 (1974): 187–90.
[23]E. Netzer, *Israel Exploration Journal* 25 (1975): 89–100; E. Netzer and E.M. Meyers, BASOR 228 (1977): 1–27; S.F. Singer, *Biblical Archaeology Review* 3 (1977): 1–17.

1965 under the direction of Y. Yadin cleared almost all of the site.

One of the marvels of Herod's construction was the creation of huge cisterns to hold 1,400,000 cubic feet of water. Facilities using this water included a Roman bath house and a swimming pool. At the northern end of Masada Herod built a three-tiered palace with plastered walls painted to imitate marble. The mosaic designs were all aniconic in deference to Herod's Jewish subjects. A columbarium is believed to have held ashes of Herod's Gentile soldiers.

6. *Herodium.* Herod, who died at Jericho, was buried at Herodium, 3 miles south of Bethlehem. The steep hill, rising 400 feet above the plain, had been artificially heightened by Herod. From 1962 to 1967 V. Corbo uncovered the structures at the top of the hill, including a double concentric wall, four towers, and a bath house. In 1972 E. Netzer uncovered an impressive complex of buildings at the base of the hill, including a large pool, 230 x 150 feet. The actual tomb of Herod was not found, but an ostracon with his name was recovered.

7. *Hebron.* Though it is not mentioned by Josephus, the finely drafted masonry of the building above Sarah's burial cave at Hebron is clearly a work of Herod's craftsmen. Two miles north of Hebron at Ramat el-Khalil, the site of Mamre, an unfinished Herodian enclosure was rebuilt by Hadrian.

Qumran

Khirbet Qumran, the ruins of the monastery, is located a half mile south of Cave I, where the first of the Dead Sea Scrolls were discovered. Excavations were conducted here from 1951 to 1956 under G.L. Harding and R. de Vaux.[24]

The major settlement that can be associated with the MSS from the caves began in the time of Hyrcanus I (134–104 B.C.). The site was abandoned after the earthquake of 31 B.C. and reoccupied at the time of Herod's death in 4 B.C. Although no texts were found, pottery similar to that in which MSS were stored in Cave I were found. One sherd was used by a budding scribe to practice writing the alphabet. Several hundred coins that were found helped date the occupation levels.

The main settlement covered an area about 260 feet square. Two hundred to four hundred persons may have lived at Qumran at one time. Most of them must have lived in huts or tents outside the buildings. A few lived in nearby caves, where signs of occupation have been found.

The most striking feature of the Khirbet is the number of cisterns and pools found there, some of which may have been used for the ritual immersions of members of the sect. A plastered aqueduct from a mountain to the west supplied the cisterns with water.[25]

Low plaster tables (or benches) and inkwells were found. These came from the scriptorium, the room used for copying MSS. The largest room, 72 feet long, served as the refectory for the communal meals of the sect.

Some 2 miles to the south of the Khirbet, farm buildings were uncovered by the spring of 'Ain Feshka.

Between the Khirbet and the Dead Sea there was a

---

[24]R. de Vaux, *Archaeology and the Dead Sea Scrolls* (New York: Oxford University Press, 1973).

[25]For an interpretation of the occupation periods with a history of the Essenes, see J. Murphy-O'Connor, BA 40 (1977): 121–24. Most scholars identify the Qumranians as Essenes.

sizeable cemetery with over one thousand burials. R. de Vaux excavated forty-three of these and found skeletons of women and children as well as men. In 1966–67 S. Steckoll uncovered ten additional skeletons.

In 1969 P. Bar-Adon discovered a site of 'Ain Ghuweir, 9 miles south of Qumran, where he uncovered a banquet hall. He also uncovered twenty burials and found a jar with the same script as that used in the Dead Sea Scrolls.[26]

John the Baptist

Inasmuch as John the Baptist grew up in the same area of the wilderness of Judea, was an ascetic, and practiced immersion as the Qumranian sect did, not a few scholars have associated the Baptist with the Qumran community. There are, however, striking differences that make such an association problematic.[27]

Luke's reference (3:1) to "Lysanias tetrarch of Abilene" at the beginning of John's ministry in the fifteenth year of Tiberius was for a long time held to be a chronological error because the only ruler of that name known from ancient sources was a Lysanias executed in 36 B.C. Two Greek inscriptions from Abila, northwest of Damascus, now prove that there was a "Lysanias the tetrarch" between the years A.D. 14 and 29. Luke's additional reference to "Philip tetrarch of Iturea and Trachonitis" is corroborated by an inscription from Seeia.

For denouncing the illicit union of Herod Antipas and Herodias, John the Baptist was imprisoned and ulti-

[26]*Revue Biblique* 77 (1970): 398–400.

[27]W.S. LaSor, *The Dead Sea Scrolls and the New Testament* (Grand Rapids: Eerdmans, 1972), pp. 142–53; C. Scobie, *John the Baptist* (Philadelphia: Fortress, 1964), pp. 135–39.

mately beheaded. According to Josephus, the scene of his imprisonment was the Herodian fortress of Machaerus, 4 miles east of the Dead Sea. In 1968 J. Vardaman conducted a brief expedition to Machaerus. He noted Herodian bath installations and aqueducts.

Jesus of Nazareth

1. *The Christmas census.* One of the most controversial questions as to the accuracy of Luke concerns the Christmas census (Luke 2:2). It is quite certain that Jesus was born before 4 B.C., the date of the death of Herod the Great. Now a census under Quirinius as governor of Syria is well known for A.D. 6 but none is known for the period before 4 B.C.

W.M. Ramsay attempted to interpret a Latin inscription as a reference to an earlier service of Quirinius as an extraordinary legate for military purposes. The view that Quirinius served before A.D. 6 has been accepted by J. Finegan,[28] but has been rejected by other scholars.[29] The fact remains, however, that Luke was well aware of the famous later census under Quirinius in A.D. 6—a census that provoked the revolt of Judas of Galilee (Acts 5:37).

2. *Bethlehem.* When we examine the places associated with Jesus, we find that we are often dependent on late traditions. In A.D. 70 Jerusalem was destroyed by Titus, and again in 135 by Hadrian, who made the city the pagan Aelia Capitolina, which was forbidden territory for any

---

[28]J. Finegan, *Handbook of Biblical Chronology* (Princeton: Princeton University Press, 1964), p. 238.

[29]E.g., A.N. Sherwin-White, *Roman Society and Roman Law in the New Testament* (Oxford: Clarendon, 1963), pp. 162–71.

Jews or Christians of Jewish origin. A Gentile Christian community did, however, live on in Jerusalem during this period.

The tradition that Jesus was born at Bethlehem in a cave goes back to Justin Martyr, who was born c. 100 in Neapolis in Samaria. Jerome, who translated the Vulgate, made his home in an adjacent cave in 385. He tells us that Hadrian had desecrated the cave of the nativity by consecrating it with a grove of Tammuz-Adonis and that Constantine's mother Helena had built a church over the site in 326. The present Church of the Holy Nativity is a basilica built by Justinian (sixth century). Investigations in 1934 and 1948–51 have revealed floor mosaics below the present floor that belong to the Constantinian church.

Just east of Bethlehem, V. Tzaferis discovered a well-preserved fourth-century A.D. church in 1972 at Beit Sahur, the Greek Orthodox site of the shepherds' fields (Luke 2:8–18). The earliest chapel was a natural cave paved with mosaics.

3. *Nazareth.* Nazareth, where Jesus spent his childhood, is not mentioned in the OT, the Talmud, or Josephus. Its name on an epigraphic source was first discovered by Avi-Yonah in 1962 on a fragment from Caesarea describing the twenty-four courses of the priestly rotation (cf. Luke 1:5).[30]

Of the holy sites at Nazareth, none seems to be of certain association except Mary's well, which is fed by the only good spring in Nazareth. Excavations by Bagatti from 1955 to 1960 beneath the Church of the Annunciation revealed what the excavator interprets as a fourth-

---

[30]M. Avi-Yonah in Vardaman, *The Teacher's Yoke* (note 1), pp. 46–57.

century synagogue-church of Jewish Christians. Graffiti include such phrases as "Rejoice Mary," and "On the holy place of M[ary] I have written there."

4. *Capernaum.* The identification of the site of Tell Hum on the northwest shore of the Sea of Galilee as Capernaum (Kfar Nahum, "Village of Nahum") is certain. In the first century A.D. the town extended 250 yards along the shore and 500 yards inland and had a population of about a thousand.

The famous synagogue was first identified in 1866. It was excavated in 1905 by H. Kohl and C. Watzinger. They dated the building to A.D. 200. G. Orfali, who worked at the site from 1921 to 1926, argued that it was the actual synagogue where Jesus taught (Mark 1:21; Luke 4:31–37). V. Corbo and S. Loffreda, who conducted investigations from 1968 to 1972, now date the extant building to the fourth century A.D. on the basis of thousands of coins found in sealed places.[31] In the southeast corner, below the limestone steps, are black basalt blocks that may possibly belong to the synagogue of Jesus' day.

The main building was originally two stories high with a staircase to the rear. Orfali's conjecture that the upper gallery was used by women has been refuted by Safrai, who notes that such segregated galleries date only from the Middle Ages.[32]

The institution of the synagogue is commonly derived from the experience of the exiled Jews in Mesopotamia. But the earliest actual epigraphic evidence for synagogues dates from c. 250 B.C. and comes from Egypt. Remains of about twenty synagogues have been

---

[31]R. North, *Biblica* 58 (1977): 424–31.
[32]In Safrai, *The Jewish People* (note 8), p. 939.

uncovered in the Diaspora, most notably the richly decorated synagogue at Dura Europos (A.D. 245). In Palestine remains of more than one hundred synagogues have been identified, almost all of them from the Late Roman and the Byzantine eras (A.D. 300–600).

5. *Chorazin.* Just inland from Capernaum is the site of Chorazin, the town that was severely reproached by Jesus (Matt 11:20–21). There is a basalt synagogue here of the second to third century, with a "seat of Moses" (Matt 23:2) for the chief official of the synagogue.[33] Similar chairs have been found at the synagogues of Hammath-Tiberias and of Delos.

6. *Magdala.* Just south of Capernaum is the site of Magdala, the home of Mary Magdalene. Recent excavations have identified its harbor and uncovered two Roman streets and a small synagogue (first century A.D.) with five stone benches seating only thirty persons.

7. *Kursi.* Jesus' exorcism of the so-called Gadarene demoniac has been a problem because of the textual variants of the name of the site (Matt 8:28; Mark 5:1; Luke 8:26). Archaeology has now shed some light on this textual problem. Origen's comment that there was an old town on the eastern shore of the Sea of Galilee was confirmed in the course of road-building operations in 1970. D. Urman has excavated a first-century A.D. fishing harbor

---

[33]In the same passage (Matt 23:5) Jesus denounced the Pharisees for making their phylacteries (*tefillin*) broad. The actual phylacteries recovered from Qumran are quite small. See Y. Yadin, *Tefillin From Qumran* (Jerusalem: Israel Exploration Society, 1969).

called Kursi in Jewish sources, and a fourth-century church, which commemorated the site of the miracle.[34]

8. *Sychar.* Mid-way between Galilee and Judea in Samaria is a site authorities believe to be fully authentic. This is Jacob's Well at Sychar where Jesus spoke with the woman of Samaria. As John's narrative describes it, the well is deep—about 100 feet. Above the site loom the twin mountains of Ebal and Gerizim. It was the latter the woman pointed out as the sacred place of worship for the Samaritans (John 4:20). The remains of the Samaritan sanctuary were visible from Sychar.[35]

9. *Pools in Jerusalem.* In Jerusalem there are two pools of water that can with confidence be associated with Jesus' ministry. The first is the pool of Siloam (John 9:7) to which Jesus sent a blind man. This is located at the end of Hezekiah's famous tunnel.

The other pool is that of Bethesda, the pool with five porches (John 5:1-4). In 1888, as the White Fathers cleared some ruins of the Church of St. Anne north of the temple area, they found an old fresco representing the story of John 5. Below this a flight of steps led down to twin pools surrounded by a portico. The northern pool was found to be about 150 feet long. M. Avi-Yonah, however, believes that the original pool sanctuary was located in a cave to the east of these remains.[36]

10. *Bethany.* The village of Bethany, just to the east of

---

[34]*Christian News From Israel* 22 (1971): 72–76.
[35]R.J. Bull, NTS 23 (1977): 460–62.
[36]M. Avi-Yonah, ed., *Encyclopedia of Archaeological Excavations in the Holy Land* (London: Oxford University Press, 1976), II, p. 608.

Jerusalem, is to day called El-Azariyeh in memory of Lazarus. The traditional tomb of Lazarus was mentioned by the Pilgrim of Bordeaux (A.D. 333). Excavations that were conducted under S.J. Saller from 1949 to 1953 showed that a church was first built near the tomb c. A.D. 390.

11. *The Cenacle.* The traditional site of the Last Supper, the second-story room of the Cenacle on "Mount Zion" is only a construction of the Franciscans in the fourteenth century. A stairway descending from Mount Zion to the Kidron Valley (John 18:1) has been uncovered on the grounds of the Church of Ṣt. Peter Gallicantu ("of the crowing cock"). This may possibly date to the reign of Herod Agrippa I (A.D. 40–44).

12. *Residences of the high priests.* The Assumptionist Fathers believe that their Church of St. Peter Gallicantu is the site of the residence of Caiaphas, the high priest who tried Jesus (Matt 26:57). Most scholars favor a site farther up Mount Zion near the Cenacle complex. The traditional site of the House of Annas, the high priest emeritus (John 18:13), is in the Armenian Quarter of the present walled city. This tradition goes back, however, only to the fourteenth century.

The Upper City of Jerusalem, where the wealthy Sadducean high priests lived, is in the Jewish Quarter of the walled city of Jerusalem. Excavations under N. Avigad since 1969 have uncovered evidence of "how the wealthy lived."[37] In one of the houses Avigad found a stone weight inscribed with the name Bar Kathros, one of the priestly families the Talmud accused of exploiting the people.

---

[37]N. Avigad, *Biblical Archaeology Review* 2 (1976): 1, 22ff.; for common dwellings, see H.K. Beebe, BA 38 (1975): 89–104.

One well-preserved Herodian house covered 2,000 square feet and had a central courtyard with four ovens. Near a stairway leading down to a cistern was a depression for washing one's feet. Signs of wealth included imported terra sigillata ware, expensive glass vessels, stone tables, mosaic pavements, and multi-colored frescoes. One fresco depicted the lampstand of the temple.

On the traditional site of the House of Caiaphas, M. Broshi in 1971–72 uncovered remains of a house with frescoes depicting representations of birds. The frescoes are similar in style to the frescoes of Pompeii.[38]

Outside the present wall between the Zion Gate and the Dung Gate, M. Ben-Dov has cleared additional buildings that are equipped with ritual baths.

13. *The trial.* The governor of Judea who condemned Jesus to be crucified was Pontius Pilate (A.D. 26–36). In 1961 A. Frova discovered in the theater at Caesarea an inscription of Pilate referring to a building he had erected in honor of Tiberius.[39]

In 1856 Father Ratisbonne bought the area near the so-called *Ecce Homo* arch for the Sisters of Zion because this was believed to be the beginning of the Via Dolorosa where Pilate said, "Behold the Man!" Later investigations showed that the arch was part of Hadrian's triple arch dated to A.D. 135.

Excavations under the Convent of the Sisters of Zion by H. Vincent in the 1930s uncovered huge striated flagstones that the excavator ascribed to the Fortress Antonia, built by Herod and named in honor of Mark Antony. The stones marked with games carved out by

---

[38]M. Broshi, *Israel Exploration Journal* 26 (1976): 84–85.
[39]J. Vardaman, JBL 81 (1962): 70–71.

Roman soldiers recall the *lithostroton* or "pavement" (John 19:13) where Jesus was tried by Pilate.[40]

P. Benoit, however, has argued from the literary references that the governor's residence where the trial was held should be located at Herod's palace in the Citadel area. He further contends that the remains under the Sisters of Zion Convent are Hadrianic rather than Herodian in date.[41]

14. *The Crucifixion.* Pilate had Jesus scourged (John 19:1) with a brutal whip embedded with bits of bone or lumps of lead. Excavators have found the head of such a whip at Heshban in Jordan.

In 1968 the first physical evidence of crucifixion was found in an ossuary from Giv'at at ha-Mivtar in northeastern Jerusalem. The ossuary, which dates between A.D. 6 and 66, contained the heel bones of a young man named Johanan still transfixed by a four-and-a-half-inch iron nail. A crease in the radial bone shows that the victim had been nailed in his forearms not in the palms as in traditional paintings of Christ's crucifixion (*cheir* in John 20:27 can mean "arm"). Johanan's leg bones had been shattered to hasten his death as had been done to the malefactors who were crucified with Jesus (John 19:31–32).[42]

15. *The tomb of Christ.* The traditional site of Calvary and the associated tomb of Christ was desecrated by Hadrian in A.D. 135. In the fourth century, Helena, the mother of

[40]Marie Aline de Sion, *La forteresse Antonia à Jérusalem et la question du prétoire* (Jerusalem: Franciscan Printing Press, 1955).

[41]P. Benoit, *Harvard Theological Review* 64 (1971): 135–67; idem, *Australian Journal of Biblical Archaeology* 1 (1973): 16–22.

[42]N. Haas, *Israel Exploration Journal* 20 (1970): 38–59; cf. M. Hengel, *Crucifixion* (London: SCM, 1977).

Constantine, was led to the site, where she then built the Church of the Holy Sepulchre. Excavations in and around the church have helped demonstrate that it lay outside the wall in Jesus' day. Shafts dug in the church show that the area was used as a quarry and was therefore extramural, a conclusion also supported by Kenyon's excavations in the adjoining Muristan area. Thus there is no reason to doubt the general authenticity of the site.

In the course of repairs since 1954 remains of the original Constantinian structure have been exposed.[43] In 1975 M. Broshi found near St. Helena's chapel in the church a red and black picture of a Roman sailing ship and a Latin phrase *Domine ivimus* "Lord, we went" (cf. Ps 122:1). These words and the drawing were placed there by a pilgrim c. A.D. 330.[44]

As for the actual tomb of Christ, quarrying operations may have obliterated the grave.[45] A bench *arcosolium* (flat surface under a recessed arch) must have been used for Jesus. But early Christian pilgrims seem to have seen a trough *arcosolium* (rock-cut sarcophagus); this raises the question of whether they saw the actual tomb.[46]

In 1842 Otto Thenius, a German pastor, was attracted to a hill 150 yards north of the present walled city because of two cavities that gave it a skull-like appearance. The hill was popularized among Protestants as an alternative site for Calvary by General Gordon in 1883. A seventeenth-century sketch of the hill demonstrates, however, that the cavities were not yet present then. The nearby

---

[43]C. Coüasnon, *The Church of the Holy Sepulchre in Jerusalem* (London: Oxford University Press, 1974).

[44]M. Broshi, *Biblical Archaeology Review* 3 (1977): 42–44.

[45]K.J. Conant, *Proceedings of the American Philosophical Society* 102 (1958): 16.

[46]J.P. Kane, *Religion* 2 (1972): 60.

"Garden Tomb" likewise has no claim to be the authentic tomb of Christ.

Tombs that were closed with disc-shaped stones rolling in a channel may be seen at the Herodian family tomb near the King David Hotel and at the so-called Tomb of the Kings, actually the richly decorated tomb of Queen Helen of Adiabene. Recently such tombs have also been discovered at Heshban in Jordan.

A long Aramaic inscription discovered at Giv'at ha-Mivtar describes how a man named Abba buried another man named Mattathiah in a tomb, reminding us of the good deed of Joseph of Arimathea, who buried Jesus in his tomb (Matt 27:57–60).[47] In 1930 a Greek inscription, purportedly from Nazareth, was published in which an emperor, probably Claudius, sternly warned against damaging tombs, exhuming the dead, and transporting the dead from one tomb to another (cf. Matt 28:12–13). Bruce tentatively suggests the possibility that Claudius, "antiquarian as he was," may have heard about the rumors of Jesus' empty tomb and have concluded that it was the result of tomb spoliation.[48]

16. *Ossuary inscriptions.* Prior to A.D. 70 it was often customary to rebury the bones of the dead in ossuaries. We now have about 250 ossuary inscriptions in Hebrew, Aramaic, and Greek.

The discovery in 1931 of an ossuary with the name in Aramaic "Jesus, son of Joseph" created a sensation, until Sukenik—the great Jewish authority—quickly denied that this had anything to do with Jesus of Nazareth. At least six ossuaries with the name Jesus are now known; Josephus

---

[47]E.S. Rosenthal, *Israel Exploration Journal* 23 (1973): 72–81.

[48]F.F. Bruce, *New Testament History* (Garden City, N.Y.: Doubleday, 1972), pp. 300–303.

mentions no less than twenty persons with the name Jesus.

In 1874 C. Clermont-Ganneau reported the discovery of burials that yielded the names Mary, Martha, and Eleazar (Lazarus). Between 1953 and 1955 B. Bagatti conducted excavations on the grounds of Dominus Flevit ("The Lord Wept") on the slopes of the Mount of Olives. He recovered forty-three inscriptions with many of the same names as are found in the NT. Many of these names, however, are quite common: Simon occurs thirty-two times, Joseph twenty-one times, Mary eighteen times, Martha eleven times, etc.

Though many of the ossuaries bear cross marks, this does not demonstrate that these are Christian burials, inasmuch as clearly Jewish ossuaries, e.g., that of Nicanor, also bear such marks. The cross on Jewish ossuaries may represent the letter Taw (cf. Ezek 9:4) as a mark of those faithful to the Lord.

But in one case from Dominus Flevit what is inscribed seems to be the Chi-Rho symbol (☧) for "Christ" or "Christian." Inscribed on another is a monogram of the Greek letters Iota, Chi, and Beta, standing perhaps for "*Iēsous Christos Boēthia*" ("Help!").[49]

Two ossuary inscriptions discovered in Talpioth, a southern suburb of Jerusalem, were called the "earliest records of Christianity" by Sukenik.[50] A coin of Agrippa I and pottery indicate that the ossuaries belong to the period before A.D. 50. The two ossuaries bear the enigmatic inscriptions in Greek: *IĒSOU IOU* and *IĒSOU ALŌTH*. These were interpreted by Sukenik as cries of

---

[49]J. Finegan, *The Archaeology of the New Testament* (Princeton: Princeton University Press, 1969), pp. 248–49.

[50]E.L. Sukenik, AJA (1947): 351–65.

lamentation addressed to Jesus. Kane, on the other hand, interprets these as simple personal names.[51] He does concede the possibility that the ossuary of Alexander of Cyrene, son of Simon, may be that of the son of the man who carried Jesus' cross (Mark 15:21).[52]

The Apostle Paul

1. *The synagogue of the freedmen.* A Greek inscription that may have belonged to the synagogue of the "libertines"— i.e., freedmen or former slaves—mentioned in Acts 6:9 was found by R. Weill in 1914 on the Ophel hill in Jerusalem.[53] The text mentions a Theodotos and his family who had built a synagogue and lodgings for Jews from the Diaspora. His father's name indicates that he was at one time a Roman slave.

Although the Jews in the Diaspora were generally lax in their observance of their religion, this was not true of Diaspora Jews like Theodotus and Saul of Tarsus who were so zealous for their faith that they emigrated to Jerusalem.

2. *Damascus.* Following his dramatic conversion, Saul came to the city of Damascus. The course of "the Street called Straight" (Acts 9:11) is still preserved by Darb al-Mustaqim (Bab Sharqi) Street. In 1947 the Syrians discovered a Roman arch about 13 feet below the present level. The eastern triple gate at the end of the street also dates from the Roman period.

[51]J.P. Kane, *Palestine Exploration Quarterly* 103 (1971): 103–8.
[52]Kane, *Religion* 2 (1972): 68.
[53]A. Deissmann, *Light from the Ancient East* (Grand Rapids: Baker, 1965 reprint of 1922 ed.), p. 440.

Saul escaped from Damascus and eluded the grasp of Aretas, who guarded the gate (2 Cor 11:32). This was Aretas IV (9 B.C.–A.D. 40), the king of the Nabataeans whose capital was Petra. He was the father-in-law of Herod Antipas. Inscriptions of this king have been found in Avdat in Palestine, Sidon in Phoenicia, and Puteoli in Italy.

3. *Paul's first missionary journey.* On his first journey Paul landed at Salamis on Cyprus and proceeded to Paphos. Extensive Roman ruins—including a gymnasium, theater, and amphitheater—are visible in Salamis. Polish excavators since 1965 have cleared a magnificent Roman palace at Nea Paphos.[54] At least one inscription found on Cyprus may be attributed to Sergius Paulus (Acts 13:7), the governor who was converted after hearing the Word of the Lord from Paul.[55]

Paul and Barnabas then proceeded to the southern coast of Turkey, and went inland, preaching the gospel in a number of cities.

At Perga, 7 miles from the coast (Acts 13:13–14), excavations have been conducted since 1967. Paul would have seen the Hellenistic towers and the magnificent town wall. The central avenue leading to the acropolis is 90 feet wide. A large food market over 200 feet square has been uncovered.

After the missionaries healed a lame man, the populace of Lystra worshiped Barnabas as Zeus and Paul as Hermes (Acts 14:12). Inscriptions with dedications to

---

[54]P. Villiers, *Archéologia* 107 (1977): 25–33.

[55]B. Van Elderen in *Apostolic History and the Gospel*, ed. W.W. Gasque and R.P. Martin (Grand Rapids: Eerdmans, 1970), pp. 151–56.

Zeus and to Hermes have been found in the vicinity of Lystra.

The discovery of inscriptions by M. Ballance in 1956 and by B. Van Elderen in 1962 have made probable the location of Derbe (Acts 14:20) at the site of Kerti Hüyük, a 65-foot-high mound.[56]

4. *Paul's second missionary journey.* On the second journey, Paul, Silas, and Timothy were directed through the interior of Anatolia to the seaport city of Alexandria Troas, 10 miles south of the famed city of Troy. They were joined there by Luke. This important city, which once held thirty thousand inhabitants, is unexcavated. Because of looting and quarrying activities, even fewer remains are visible today than were to be seen in the eighteenth century.[57]

When Paul crossed over to Neapolis, he was not conscious of the implications of bringing the gospel to Europe. Some 8 miles from the coast was Philippi, famed for the battle between Antony and Octavian's forces and the assassins of Caesar in 42 B.C. Luke's use of the Greek word *meris* (Acts 16:12) to mean a "region" was held to be an error till papyri from Egypt demonstrated that colonists from Macedonia idiomatically used the word with this meaning.

One of Paul's converts was Lydia, a seller of purple cloth from Thyatira. In 1872 a text was found reading, "The city honored from among the purple-dyers, an outstanding citizen, Antiochus the son of Lykus, a native of Thyatira, as a benefactor." Excavations by the French since 1914 have uncovered Roman shops around the forum and a fourth-century basilica on the little river to

---

[56]Ibid., pp. 156–61.
[57]C.J. Hemer, *Tyndale Bulletin* 26 (1975): 79–112.

the east, commemorating the site of the gathering in which Lydia participated (Acts 16:13).

Paul, Silas, and Timothy traveled from Philippi 75 miles west to Thessalonica on the famous Via Egnatia, parts of which are still visible. Luke's accuracy is again attested when he speaks of the *politarchs* of Thessalonica (Acts 17:6). As this term was not found in any classical author, Luke's use of the word was suspect. But the term has been found in at least seventeen inscriptions from the area of Thessalonica. Recent excavations have cleared a large forum, 210 by 330 feet, with buildings of the first or early second century A.D.

Paul preached his famous sermon in Athens either on the Areopagus (Mars Hill), a low hill below the Acropolis, or to the Areopagus Court, which sometimes met in the Royal Stoa.[58] In 1969 excavations north of the Athens-Piraeus railroad uncovered a small building that has been identified as the Royal Stoa. Hemer has suggested that it was here that Paul spoke to the Areopagus Court, in the very same site where Socrates once confronted his accuser.[59] Paul's reference to an inscription "TO AN UNKNOWN GOD" (Acts 17:23) has been illustrated by an inscription found at Pergamum dedicated to the "Unknown Gods."

Paul's ministry at Corinth has been richly illuminated by excavations. In the agora may be seen the *bema* or "judgment seat" before which Paul was tried (Acts 18:12–17). Paul's judge was Gallio, the brother of Seneca. Fragments of a stone inscription of Claudius found at Delphi refer to Gallio as the "Proconsul of Achaea." As the text

---

[58]R.E. Wycherley, *The Stones of Athens* (Princeton: Princeton University Press, 1978), p. 31.

[59]C.J. Hemer, NTS 20 (1973–74): 341–50.

is dated to A.D. 52, it fixes the date of Paul's stay in Corinth.

Near the theater was found an inscription that refers to the donation of a pavement by an *aedile,* or commissioner of public works, named Erastus. It is probable that this is the same Erastus who was Paul's co-worker (Acts 19:22) and who is also called the "manager" of the city (Rom 16:23).

In 1898 excavators found a broken Greek inscription that can be restored to read: "(Syna)gogue of the (Hebr)ews." Its crude lettering may indicate either the low social level of the Jews of Corinth or a late date. A marble fragment with a menorah has also been found.

The congregation at Corinth was endangered by immorality and by disputes over meats offered in pagan rituals. High above the city on the Acrocorinth stood the temple of Aphrodite with more than a thousand sacred prostitutes.[60] A thorough investigation of the Acrocorinth by C. Blegen in 1926 revealed some finely worked poros blocks that may have come from Aphrodite's temple.

Inscriptions found at the base of the Acrocorinth and in the theater testify to a flourishing cult of the Egyptian gods Isis and Serapis in the first century A.D. Recent excavations of the sanctuary of Demeter on the Acrocorinth have uncovered small theaters for religious spectacles and rooms with stone couches for cultic meals. Such rooms have also been found in the area of the Asclepius sanctuary north of the forum.

About 6 miles east of Corinth was Isthmia, the site of pan-Hellenic games attended by Nero and probably by Paul. O. Broneer has excavated the sanctuary of Poseidon, which also featured caves with cultic dining rooms. Paul's

---

[60]Cf. E. Yamauchi in *Orient and Occident,* ed. H. Hoffner (Kevelaer: Butzon & Bercker, 1973), pp. 213–22.

reference to a "corruptible crown" (1 Cor 9:25) can be illustrated by a stone head carved with a crown of pine leaves from Isthmia and by a mosaic of an athlete with a crown of celery leaves from Corinth.

Corinth had harbors on either side of the isthmus. Paul no doubt used the eastern harbor at Cenchreae, which was Phoebe's home (Rom 16:1). Warehouses from the first century A.D. have recently been uncovered at this port.

5. *Paul's third missionary journey.* Paul's third mission was spent largely at Ephesus in western Asia Minor. The city's greatest claim to fame was the temple of Artemis (Roman Diana), one of the seven wonders of the world and the largest edifice of the Hellenistic world. The remains of the temple were found by a persistent English architect who searched for seven years. Very little remains to be seen of the temple at the site today; one of the pillars is on display at the British Museum. Some idea of the appearance of the temple may be obtained from its depiction on coins.[61] An even better idea may be gained by viewing the well-preserved temple of Apollo at Didyma; this was designed by the same architect and was only slightly smaller than the Artemision of Ephesus.

Ephesus has been excavated by Austrian archaeologists since 1896. In 1965 they discovered near the site of the temple a horseshoe-shaped altar that dates back to 700 B.C.[62]

The great theater (Acts 19:29–31) where the angry Ephesians met to protest Paul's preaching held as many

---

[61]B. Trell, *The Temple of Artemis at Ephesus* (New York: The American Numismatic Society, 1945).

[62]A. Bammer, *Archaeology* 27.3 (1974): 202–5.

as twenty-four thousand persons. On the Street of the Curetes not far from the theater excavations in 1967 uncovered a house that was decorated with theatrical scenes from Menander's comedies and Euripides' tragedies. Paul may not have attended the theater but he was able to quote from Menander's play *Thais* (1 Cor 15:33).

It was especially the silversmiths (Acts 19:24ff.) who saw in Paul a threat to their business of making silver statues of Artemis. A Demetrius who is mentioned in an inscription may be the same as the ringleader of the riot.[63] An inscription in Greek and Latin from the theater describes the dedication of silver images of Artemis by a Roman official. A recently discovered inscription sheds further light on the intense devotion given to Artemis of Ephesus. It records that forty-five inhabitants of Sardis who maltreated a sacred embassy from Ephesus bearing cloaks for Artemis were condemned to die.[64]

From about 150 B.C. the goddess is depicted with several rows of bulbous objects on her chest, usually interpreted as breasts. Other scholars have interpreted the round objects as ostrich eggs, which were symbols of fertility, or as astrological symbols.[65] Statues of the goddess have been found at Hierapolis, Laodicea, Colosse, and even at Caesarea in Palestine.

Evidence of the Jewish community may be seen in a menorah carved in the steps leading up to the second-century A.D. Library of Celsus. Several lamps with the menorah design were found in the Cemetery of the Seven Sleepers.

---

[63]Sherwin-White, p. 91.

[64]F. Sokolowski, *Harvard Theological Review* 58 (1965): 427–31.

[65]R. Fleischer, *Artemis von Ephesos und verwandte Kultstatuen aus Anatolien und Syrien* (Leiden: Brill, 1973), pp. 74–97.

After revisiting the churches in Macedonia and in Achaia, Paul sailed back to Troas and then walked to Assos (Acts 20:13). This coastal city, where Aristotle once stayed, was excavated from 1881 to 1883. The walls, still standing nearly 50 feet high, are the best preserved fortifications of the Hellenistic world.

Paul next came to Miletus, a great Ionian city famed for its philosophers and its colonies. Excavations begun by Germans in 1899 were intensified after 1955, when an earthquake destroyed the village that rested over part of the site. The theater at Miletus could seat more than fifteen thousand people. Two of the columns that supported the imperial baldachin, or canopy, are still standing. An inscription in the fifth row marks the seats reserved for the "Jews and the God-fearing" proselytes.[66]

Other remains unearthed at Miletus include the two lion statues that guarded the main harbor, extensive stoas (colonnaded porches), and a synagogue. The north gateway of the southern Agora has been restored in the East Berlin Museum.

On his return voyage Paul stopped at the Lycian port of Patara. Ruins that can still be seen there are the city wall, a triple gate, baths of Vespasian, and a granary erected by Hadrian. Outstanding is a theater that dates from the time of Tiberius and was refurbished in A.D. 147.

6. *Paul's voyage to Rome.* After being held in prison at Caesarea for two years under Felix and then Festus, Paul took advantage of his status as a Roman citizen to appeal to Caesar in Rome. Felix was a Greek freedman, whose brother Pallas was in charge of Nero's treasury. In 1966

---

[66]H. Hommel, *Instanbuler Mitteilungen* 25 (1975): 167–93.

the first epigraphical reference to Felix was found 10 miles north of Caesarea.[67]

As it left the southwestern coast of Anatolia, Paul's ship sailed by the narrow isthmus of Cnidus (Acts 27:7). Excavations by Iris Love since 1967 have uncovered the ancient harbor, warehouses, and the round temple of Aphrodite Euploia (of Good Sailing) where once stood Praxitiles' sensational nude statue of the goddess.

After Paul's ship was wrecked on the coast of Malta, the survivors were lodged in the house of Publius, "the chief man of the island" (Acts 28:7). His title has been confirmed by Greek and Latin inscriptions from the island.

7. *Paul's arrival in Italy.* Paul landed at Puteoli on the Bay of Naples (Acts 28:13).[68] There he saw Mount Vesuvius, the volcano that was to bury Herculaneum and Pompeii in 79. This disaster has preserved gladiatorial barracks, palatial villas with their paintings, and the contorted forms of men and animals. Bronze statues, medical instruments, furniture, and carbonized food have been recovered.

The trace of a cruciform object at Herculaneum has been interpreted as evidence of a Christian chapel.[69] Two copies of an anagram from Pompeii that can spell *Pater Noster* ("Our Father") have also been interpreted as

---

[67]According to the restoration of M. Avi-Yonah, *Israel Exploration Journal* 16 (1966): 258–64.

[68]The site of Ostia at the mouth of the Tiber River was developed as a major port by Claudius, Trajan, and Hadrian. The well-preserved ruins include remains of *insulae* (apartment buildings), warehouses, and numerous Mithraea.

[69]J. Deiss, *Herculaneum* (New York: Crowell, 1970), pp. 65, 69.

possible evidence of Christianity. Either a Jew or a Christian scribbled "SODOMA, GOMORRA" at Pompeii.[70]

Among the remains of structures Paul saw when he arrived in Rome are those of the Basilica Julia and the temple of the Vestal Virgins, the Altar of Peace and the Mausoleum of Augustus, and the theater of Pompey, now used as an apartment building. The Curia or Senate building dates from a rebuilding by Diocletian (A.D. 303). It was only after Paul's first imprisonment and the disastrous fire that devastated Rome in 64 that Nero erected his fabulous Golden House, sections of which may still be seen.

Paul doubtless saw the great Circus Maximus, which held 250,000 spectators for the chariot races, but he could not have seen the Colosseum, which was not dedicated until 80 by Titus.

Remains of the Jewish community in Rome include references to at least thirteen synagogues. The overwhelming number of the 550 epitaphs from six catacombs are in Greek.

8. *Paul's imprisonment and burial.* The traditional site of Paul's final imprisonment is the Tullianum or Carcer Mamertinus, the state prison located below the Capitoline Hill. Behind the closed doors are two chambers one on top of the other. Famous captives such as Jugurtha and Vercingetorix were killed in the lower cell and cast into the Cloaca Maxima, the great sewer. The dank dungeon is described by Sallust as a chamber with a vaulted roof of stone: "Neglect, darkness and stench make it hideous and fearsome to behold."[71]

---

[70]P. MacKendrick, *The Mute Stones Speak* (New York: St. Martin's, 1960), pp. 218–19.

[71]M. Grant, *The Roman Forum* (London: Spring, 1970), p. 128.

Writing late in the second century, Proclus noted the monument to Paul's burial on the road from Rome to Ostia. The traditional site is marked by a white slab (fourth century) reading: "To Paul, Apostle and Martyr" within the Church of St. Paul's Outside-the-Walls.

The Apostle Peter

1. *Peter's home in Capernaum.* About 30 feet from the synagogue in Capernaum, Franciscan excavators dug under a fifth-century octagonal church. Beneath this level they found what they describe as a fourth-century synagogue church. This was built over an enlarged private house that was venerated as early as the first century A.D. On the plastered walls are some 130 graffiti in Aramaic, Greek, and Latin primarily from the third century, including references to "Peter" and "Rome." On the basis of reports by Egeria (A.D. 385) and by the Piacenza pilgrim (A.D. 570), the excavators conclude that they have found Peter's house, which was later transformed into a church.[72]

2. *Peter's ministry.* On the day of Pentecost Peter preached to Jewish pilgrims from many countries of the Diaspora (Acts 2:5–11; cf. 1 Peter 1:1). Unfortunately the archaeological evidence from the Diaspora, except for papyri from Egypt[73] and a few Hellenistic synagogues, is almost entirely dated to the third or the fourth century A.D.[74] The synagogues of Delos and Miletus are Hellenistic; that at

---

[72]V. Corbo, *The House of Saint Peter at Capharnaum* (Jerusalem: Franciscan Printing Press, 1969).

[73]Cf. V.A. Tcherikover and A. Fuks, eds., *Corpus Papyrorum Judaicarum* (Cambridge: Harvard University Press, 1957), I, pp. 25–44.

[74]M. Avi-Yonah in Safrai (note 8), I, p. 53.

Ostia rests on a building that may have been used as a synagogue in the early Roman Empire.

Inscriptions of the first century A.D. from Acmonia in Phrygia (Acts 2:10) in Turkey indicate that some of the wealthy Jews were citizens of the city. Evidence from the first century B.C. to the first century A.D. from the cemetery at Cyrene (Acts 2:10) shows that members of the Jewish aristocracy received a gymnasium education and served as magistrates.

Peter was privileged to be instrumental in the conversion of Cornelius, the centurion at Caesarea. Cornelius commanded one hundred soldiers in a cohort of six hundred men. The Italian cohort he belonged to (Acts 10:1) may have been either the Cohors II Italica Civium Romanorum, a corps of freedmen known to have been stationed in Syria, or the Cohors Augustian Auranitis that later served under Agrippa II.

3. *Peter's tomb.* Excavations were conducted by Catholic scholars under St. Peter's Church from 1939 to 1950 and from 1953 to 1957. A set of bones was produced in 1965; in 1968 Pope Paul VI announced that he was convinced these are the very bones of Peter.

What is certain is that the archaeologists uncovered an *aedicula* or memorial shrine that may be identified with the "trophy" of Peter mentioned by Gaius c. A.D. 200, which had been set up c. A.D. 160.

Pope Paul's conviction regarding the alleged bones of Peter rests on the work of Margherita Guarducci, professor of Greek epigraphy at Rome.[75] She interpreted third- and fourth-century graffiti as a crypto-language

---

[75]M. Guarducci, *The Tomb of St. Peter* (London: Harrap, 1960).

used by the faithful. Though other scholars believe that the Vatican was the area of Peter's martyrdom, they doubt that the very grave or the bones of Peter have been discovered.[76]

The Apostle John and the Churches of Revelation

The Aegean island of Patmos (Rev. 1:9) where John was exiled during the reign of Domitian contains two monasteries dedicated to the apostle but no remains from a very early period.[77] In Revelation 2-3 letters are addressed to these seven churches of western Asia Minor:

1. *Ephesus.* A number of buildings that can be ascribed to Domitian have been identified, including a huge temple dedicated to the emperor and standing on a terrace by the upper or state agora. The head and the forearm of a colossal statue of Domitian have been recovered.

In the second century a church was erected over the traditional site of John's grave on a hill outside Ephesus. Here in the sixth century Justinian built a magnificent church over 300 feet long and about 100 feet wide. Excavations at the site were conducted between 1927 and 1929, and recently considerable restoration has been done.[78]

By the fourth century a tradition developed that John had taken Jesus' mother Mary with him to Ephesus. Part of an enormous Roman building, perhaps the grain and money exchange, 850 feet long, was transformed into the

[76]G.F. Snyder, BA 32 (1969): 11-14; W. O'Connor, *Peter in Rome* (New York: Columbia University Press, 1969), p. 209.

[77]O.F.A. Meinardus, *St. John of Patmos and the Seven Churches of the Apocalypse* (Athens: Lycabettus, 1974), pp. 15-19.

[78]H. Plommer, *Anatolian Studies* 12 (1962): 119-30.

Church of the Holy Virgin c. A.D. 350. The Third Ecumenical Council was held here in A.D. 431.

2. *Smyrna.* Ancient Smyrna (modern Izmir), 35 miles north of Ephesus, was an important seaport of about two hundred thousand people. Its Hellenistic-Roman agora was excavated between 1932 and 1941. It consists of a large courtyard, 400 by 260 feet, surrounded by a two-story colonnade with a basement level.

3. *Pergamum.* The great Hellenistic city of Pergamum controlled western Asia Minor till its last king ceded his territories to Rome in 133 B.C. The city was built on a steep hill 10 miles inland from the coast.

Its greatest artistic monument, the huge altar of Zeus, was discovered in the nineteenth century and reconstructed in the Pergamum Museum of East Berlin. Some commentators have taken the statement regarding "Satan's throne" (Rev 2:13) as a reference to this altar.

Between 1878 and 1886 archaeologists cleared the upper city, including the library, which was second only to that in Alexandria. Excavations between 1900 and 1913 cleared the series of three gymnasiums on the slopes of Pergamum. At the foot of the hill is a huge building of red brick, a temple to Serapis that was converted into a church.

At some distance in the plain is the famous healing sanctuary, the Asclepion, approached by a 900-yard-long colonnaded avenue. The German excavators have cleared the sacred pools, lavatories, and rooms where patients slept in the hope of having dreams to aid them in their healing.

4. *Thyatira.* The site of Thyatira, east of Pergamum, is covered by the modern city of Akhisar. Recent excava-

tions have unearthed a second-century A.D. Roman road and stoa in the center of the town.[79]

5. *Sardis*. Sardis served as the capital of the kingdom of Lydia under the fabled Croesus till its capture by the Persians in 546 B.C. Excavations were conducted early in the twentieth century and have been resumed since 1958 under G.M.A. Hanfmann. Archaeologists have discovered evidence of gold cupellation works—a discovery that lends substance to the legend of Croesus's wealth.

The great temple of Artemis has two of its 58-foot-high columns still standing. It was built in the Hellenistic period.

Excavations have confirmed Josephus's reference to an early Jewish community at Sardis (Jos. Antiq. XIV, 259ff.) by the recovery of more than eighty Jewish inscriptions. The most spectacular discovery was an enormous synagogue, 330 feet long and 60 feet wide, which was part of a municipal gymnasium complex. The foundations for the hall go back to the second century A.D.; as restored, the synagogue dates to the fourth century. The prominence of the Jews, many of whom were goldsmiths, is shown by the fact that nine of them were members of the city council.[80] The size and prestige of the Jewish community at Sardis may help explain the vehemence of the anti-Jewish polemic of Melito, bishop of Sardis (late second century), whose sermon, *Peri Pascha*, was discovered in 1937.

[79]Meinardus, pp. 92, 100.

[80]G.M.A. Hanfmann, *Letters from Sardis* (Cambridge: Harvard University Press, 1972); idem, *From Croesus to Constantine* (Ann Arbor: University of Michigan Press, 1975).

6. *Philadelphia.* The ruins of Philadelphia are buried under the modern city of Alashehir. The theater and the stadium may have been located in the depression between the summits of the acropolis. We have inscriptional evidence for games and festivals. Marble fragments of early Byzantine churches have been found. The Church of St. John dates from a late Byzantine period.

7. *Laodicea.* Laodicea was one of the three NT cities in the Lycus valley, together with Hierapolis and Colosse (Col 4:13). Excavations between 1961 and 1963 by Laval University cleared a nymphaeum, a fountain installation.[81] Unexcavated but visible remains include a stadium dedicated in A.D. 79, two theaters, etc.

The rebuke to the church of Laodicea (Rev 3:18) refers ironically to: 1) its wealth as a banking city, 2) its famed black wool, and 3) the Phrygian eye powder of the medical school at Men Carou 30 miles away. Though the extant aqueduct was designed to bring water from the area of Denizli, 6 miles to the south, the accusation that the church was lukewarm (Rev 3:16) suggests a reference to the water of the hot springs of Hierapolis, which surely became tepid by the time it was channeled to Laodicea.[82]

The site of Hierapolis is today called Pamukkale or "Cotton Castle" because of its glistening white carbonate terraces. An Italian excavation team under Paolo Verzone has worked there since 1957. At the side of the temple of Apollo the excavators have discovered the famed Plutoni-

---

[81]J. de Gagniers, *Laodicée du Lycos* (Quebec: Université Laval, 1969); J. Maigret, M. Bobichon, P. Devambez, R. Leconte, *Bible et Terre Sainte* 81 (March, 1966): 2–16.

[82]M. Rudwick and E. Green, ExpT 69 (1957–58): 176–78.

um described by Strabo, the sulfurous-smelling entrance to the Underworld.[83]

The inhabitants of Hierapolis used an elaborate system of channels and terra-cotta pipes for the distribution of the waters of their hot springs. A colonnaded street leads to an arch of Domitian. An extensive necropolis of twelve hundred tombs with three hundred epitaphs sheds light on the Jewish and Christian communities. Jewish guilds of purple dyers (cf. Acts 16:14) and of carpet weavers are attested. An octagonal martyrium of the fifth century commemorates the martyrdom of Philip the Evangelist (Acts 21:8).

At nearby Colosse the outline of a theater and building fragments are visible, but the site itself has never been excavated.[84]

The Jewish Revolt

The dire prophecies of Jesus regarding the fate of the temple (Matt 24:1ff.; Mark 13:1ff.; Luke 21:5ff.) were fulfilled within a generation when the Jews rebelled against the Romans in A.D. 66 in the reign of Nero. The "zealot" movement, which had its beginnings in the revolt of Judas of Galilee in A.D. 6 (Acts 5:37) and had included Simon Zelotes (Luke 6:15) and Barabbas (Mark 15:7), became increasingly violent during the governorship of Felix with the rise of the *sicarii* "assassins" (Acts 21:38), who murdered Roman collaborators.

Excavations have confirmed Josephus's vivid descriptions of the horrifying events of the war in which

---

[83]G.E. Bean, *Turkey Beyond the Maeander* (London: Benn, 1971), p. 233.

[84]W.H. Mare, *Near East Archaeological Society Bulletin* 7 (1976): 39–59.

various zealot factions fought each other as well as the Romans.

At the beginning of the war Josephus was given command of Galilee. He surrendered Jotapata to the Romans under suspicious circumstances. The double defense wall and the cave openings may still be seen at the site of Yodefat just as Josephus described them. The stronghold of Gamala east of the Sea of Galilee has yielded scores of stone missiles and arrowheads from Vespasian's siege.

By A.D. 68 Vespasian had captured most of the Jordan valley, destroying the monastery at Qumran. By 69 the Jews held only the areas of Jerusalem, Herodium, Masada, and Machaerus—sites that had been fortified by Herod.

When Vespasian was proclaimed emperor in 69, he sent his son Titus to consult the oracle of Venus (Aphrodite) on Cyprus. Excavators at Nea Paphos in 1968 recovered from a cistern an oval gem with the inscription of the XVth Legion Apollinaris; it must have fallen from the ring of one of Titus's officers on this occasion.

In narrating the siege of Jerusalem by Titus in 70, Josephus describes three northern walls. The first ran from the Citadel to the temple area. The second must have run east of the Church of the Holy Sepulchre to the Fortress Antonia. The course of the third wall, built by Herod Agrippa I, has been highly controverted. British scholars favor the line of the present north wall on the basis of masonry found at the Damascus Gate.[85] Israeli scholars favor a line of walls some 440 yards farther north, first discovered by E.L. Sukenik and L.A. Mayer in 1925.[86]

---

[85]E.W. Hamrick, BA 40 (1977): 18–23.
[86]M. Avi-Yonah, *Israel Exploration Journal* 18 (1968): 98–125; S. Ben-Arieh and E. Netzer, *Israel Exploration Journal* 24 (1974): 97–107.

Evidences of the Roman siege of Jerusalem include thick layers of ash found by Mazar and Avigad, Roman catapult balls from below the Convent of the Sisters of Zion, and the skeletal remains of a woman from a house in the Upper City. The huge ashlars that were toppled from the parapet of the Royal Stoa crashed with such force that they buckled the Herodian pavement of the road below the temple platform.

Excavators have recovered evidence of the Zealot occupation and the Roman attacks at both Herodium and Machaerus, which fell soon after the capture of Jerusalem.

The most extensive evidence comes from Masada, the last Jewish stronghold, which fell in 73. The zealots built a synagogue, installed ritual baths, and established a hall for religious study. Under the floor of the synagogue copies of disused Scriptures were found; fragments of Ben Sira, of Jubilees, and of a Qumran-type document were also found. The zealots set up crude living quarters on the luxurious mosaic floors of Herod's palace and also in the 4,250-foot-long casemate walls surrounding the plateau. That even the zealot women were conscious of their appearance is proved by their cosmetic equipment. Over four thousand coins were recovered, including silver shekels minted by the Jewish rebels themselves.

At the base of Masada one can still see traces of eight Roman camps of the Xth Legion and a circumvallation wall of 3,800 yards. Against the western slope is the siege ramp built by Jewish prisoners. On the plateau are some of the 100-pound stones used by the defenders and hundreds of Roman ballista, the size of grapefruit. Of the 960 zealots who committed suicide at Masada, twenty-five skeletons were found in a cave and remains of three other victims in the northern palace. Among the 700 ostraca found is a lot with the name of the leader, Ben Jair; it may be one of the very lots used to decide who would kill the last survivors.

After the war the Romans stationed the Xth Legion Fretensis in Jerusalem. Numerous tiles with the legion's stamp have been found. Recently an inscription of the legion's commander, Lucius Flavius Silva (A.D. 73 to 80), has been found inscribed on a pillar in Jerusalem.[87] Roman governors of Judea after this period are known from other Latin inscriptions.[88]

The Flavian emperors—Vespasian and his sons Titus and Domitian—proclaimed their victory over the Jews in a series of Judaea Capta coins that depict the forlorn figure of a woman under a palm tree representing the Jewish nation. An inscription announcing the Roman victory has been recovered from the theater at Jerash in Jordan. The so-called Arch of Titus, which was actually erected by Domitian, depicts soldiers carrying the trumpets, the table of the shewbread, and the seven-branched menorah of the temple in a triumphal procession.

According to Eusebius, the Christians were warned to flee from Jerusalem to Pella, across the Jordan and south of the Sea of Galilee. Excavations by R.H. Smith at the site were cut short by the outbreak of hostilities in 1967. Smith believes that a sarcophagus based on earlier Jewish prototypes may be indirect evidence to support the tradition of the flight to Pella.[89]

[87]M. Gichon and B.H. Isaac, *Israel Exploration Journal* 24 (1974): 117–23.

[88]E.M. Smallwood, *The Jews Under Roman Rule* (Leiden: Brill, 1976), pp. 546–57.

[89]R.H. Smith, *Archaeology* 26 (1973): 250–56, idem, *Palestine Exploration Quarterly* 105 (1973): 71–82.

Bibliography

Books

Akurgal, E. *Ancient Civilizations and Ruins of Turkey.* Istanbul: Mobil Oil Türk A.S., 1970.

Avi-Yonah, M., ed. *The Herodian Period (World History of the Jewish People* VII). New Brunswick: Rutgers University Press, 1975.

Barrett, C.K. *The New Testament Background.* New York: Harper & Bros., 1961.

Blaiklock, E.M. *The Archaeology of the New Testament.* Grand Rapids: Zondervan, 1970.

Deissmann, A. *Light From the Ancient East.* Grand Rapids: Baker, 1965 reprint of 1922 ed.

Finegan, J. *The Archaeology of the New Testament.* Princeton: Princeton University Press, 1969.

Inscriptions Reveal. Jerusalem: Israel Museum, rev. ed., 1973.

Jeremias, J. *Jerusalem in the Time of Jesus.* Philadelphia: Fortress, 1969.

Jerusalem Revealed. Jerusalem: Israel Exploration Society, 1975.

Kenyon, K. *Jerusalem.* London: Thames and Hudson, 1967.

Kopp, C. *The Holy Places of the Gospels.* Freiburg: Herder, 1963.

Mazar, B. *The Mountain of the Lord.* Garden City, N.Y.: Doubleday, 1975.

Meinardus, O. *St. Paul in Greece.* Athens: Lycabettus, 1972.

Meshorer, Y. *Jewish Coins.* Tel Aviv: Am Hassefer, 1967.

Safrai, S. and Stern, M., eds. *The Jewish People in the First Century.* 2 vols. Philadelphia: Fortress, 1976.

Sherwin-White, A.N. *Roman Society and Roman Law in the New Testament.* Oxford: Clarendon, 1963.

Unger, M.F. *Archaeology and the New Testament.* Grand Rapids: Zondervan, 1962.

Yadin, Y. *Masada.* New York: Random, 1966.

Yamauchi, E. *The Stones and the Scriptures.* Philadelphia: Lippincott, 1972; London: Inter-Varsity, 1973.

Periodicals

Anatolian Studies (London: British Institute of Archaeology at Ankara).

Biblical Archaeologist (Cambridge: American Schools of Oriental Research).

Biblical Archaeology Review (Washington, D.C.).

Hesperia (Athens: American School of Classical Studies).

Israel Exploration Journal (Jerusalem: Israel Exploration Society).

Palestine Exploration Quarterly (London: Palestine Exploration Fund).

INDEX OF
CONTEMPORARY PERSONS

Aharoni, Y., 40
Albright, W. F., 30, 47, 63
Amiran, R., 71
Archer, G., 22
Avigad, N., 82, 106
Avi-Yonah, M., 71, 78, 81

Bagatti, 78, 87
Ballance, M., 90
Bar-Adon, P., 76
Barnett, 47
Baur, F. C., 63
Ben-Dov, M., 83
Benoit, P., 84
Bliss, P. J., 7
Botta, P. E., 6
Broneer, O., 92
Blegen, C., 92
Broshi, M., 71, 83, 85
Bruce, F. F., 64
Bull, R., 72-73
Bultmann, R., 64

Clermont-Ganneau, C., 87
Condor, C. R., 6
Corbo, V., 74, 79

Dibelius, M., 64
Dickie, A. C., 7

Eitan, A., 71

Finegan, J., 77
Frova, A., 83

Gasque, W. W., 65
Glueck, N., 22, 33
Gordon, General, 85
Guarducci, Margherita, 99

Hanfmann, G. M. A., 102
Harding, G. L., 75

Harnack, A., 64
Hemer, C. J., 91

Ingholt, H., 67

Kane, J. P., 88
Kelso, J. L., 73
Kenyon, I., 7, 21, 33, 47, 85
Kitchen, K., 22
Kitchener, H. H., 6
Kohl, H., 79

Layard, A. H., 6
Loffreda, S., 79
Loftus, W. K., 6
Love, Iris, 96

Macalister, R. A. S., 7
Mayer, L. A., 105
Mazar, B., 68
Meyers, E., 64
Muehsam, A., 71

Netzer, E., 73, 74

Olmstead, A. T., 64
Orfali, G., 79

Petrie, Flinders, 7
Pritchard, J. B., 73

Ramsay, Sir William, 64, 77
Reisner, G. H., 7
Robinson, Edward, 6, 45, 68

Safrai, 79
Saller, S. J., 82
Schumacher, G., 6
Sherwin-White, A. N., 64
Smith, Eli, 6
Smith, R. H., 107
Starkey, J., 47

Index of Contemporary Persons

Steckoll, S., 76
Sukenik, E. L., 87, 105

Thenius, Otto, 85
Tzaferis, V., 78

Unger, M. F., 22
Urman, D., 80

Van Elderen, B., 90
Verzone, Paolo, 103
Vogel, Eleanor K., 8
Vardaman, J., 77

Vattioni, 25
Vaux, R. de, 36, 75, 76
Vincent, H., 7, 52, 83

Warren, Charles, 6
Watzinger, C., 79
Weill, R., 88
Whitcomb, J. C., 79
Wright, G. E., 47

Yadin, Y., 32, 40, 74

Zahn, T., 64

GENERAL INDEX

Abarama, 14
Abila, 76
Abimelech, 30
Abraham: army of, 18; camels of, 18
Abram, 17
Aburahana (Abraham), 17
Abu Salabikh, 15
Achaia, 95
Acrocorinth, 92
Acropolis, 91
Adad-idri, 38
Adad-nirari III, 39
Adrammelech, 48
Aelia Capitolina, 77
Agrippa II, 99
Ahab, 32; alliance with Tyre, 36; and Assyria, 38; and Egypt, 38; and Moab, 37; palace of, 36-37; and Syria, 37
Ahaz: and Assyria, 42; idolatry of, 42
Ahlab, 41
Ai, EB, 15
'Ain Feshka, 75
'Ain Ghuweir, 76
Akhisar, 101
Alalah, 17, 26, 32, 33
Alashehir, 103
Alexander, 56
Alexander of Cyrene, 88
Alexandria of Troas, 90
Altars, horned, 34
Amarna letters, 20, 24, 27
Amman temples, 26
Amman (Jordan), 8
Amman (Philadelphia), 57
Ammon, 22, 38
Amraphel, 18
Anatolia, 65, 90, 96
Antiochus, 90
Antiochus IV (Ephiphanes), 57
Antiochus Eupator, 57
Antony, 90

Anun, 35
Aphek, 50
Aphrodite, temple of, 92
Aphrodite Euploia, temple of, 96
Apollo, temple of, 93, 103-4
Aqabah, mines of, 34
Aqueducts, 72, 75, 77
Arabia, 38, 57
Arad, 14, 34, 57
Aramaic, 50
Aram-Damascus, 38
'Araq el-Emir, 55-56, 57
Areopagus (Mars Hill), 91
Aretas IV, 89
Arioch, 18
Aristobulus III, 73
Armenian Gardens, 71
Arpad, 41
Artemis, temple of, 93, 102
Arvad, 38, 48
Asclepion, 92, 101
Asenath, 20
Ashdod, 21, 27, 44, 48, 57
Asherah, 27
Ashkelon, 18, 28, 29, 42, 48, 50
Ashurbanipal, 48, 49
Ashurnasirpal II, king of Assyria, 33
Asshur, 7, 8
Assos, 95
Assyria, and Damascus, 39, 41
Astarte, and figurines, 26
Ataroth, 37
Athens, 91
Athens-Pireaus, 91
Athlit, 55
Atshanah (Alalah), 8
Augustus, 67, 71, 72
Axes: copper, 9; iron, 30
Azariah (Uzziah), 40
Azekah, 35, 51, 52

Ba'al of Tyre, 48
Ba'al Sapon, 27

112

General Index

Babylon: destruction of, 43; exploration of, 7; fall of, 54
Babylonian Chronicle, 48, 49, 50, 54
Babylonia(ns), 51; and Judah, 50; King List, 41
Bacchides, 57
Bagoas, 55
Balatah (Sechem), 8
Bar Kathros, 82
Beersheba, 26, 34
Beitin (Bethel), 8. *See also* Bethel.
Beit Sahur, 78
Bell Beit Mirsim, 52
Belshazzar, 53, 54
Benhadad II, 38
Benhadad III, 39
Ben Jair, 107
Beth-Ammon, 48
Bethany, 81-82
Bethel, 17, 35, 53, 55
Bethesda, pool of, 81
Beth Horon, 33
Bethlehem, 67, 74, 77-78
Beth-shan, 15, 22; destruction of, 21; in EBI, 14; in the Iron Age, 28; temples of, 26
Beth-shemesh, 30, 31, 34, 35, 51, 52
Beth-Yerah, 15
Beth-Zur, 20, 29, 55, 57, 58
Black Obelisk, 38
Bronze Age: agriculture of, 17, 26; city-rulers of, 20; patriarchs and, 16; towns of, 14-15; writings in, 24
Buseirah, 8
Byblos, writings in, 25

Caesar, 90, 95
Caesarea, 55, 72-73, 78, 94
Caiaphas, the high priest, 82
Calah (Nimrud), 6, 33, 38, 43
Calvary, 85
Cambyses, 54
Camels, EB, 18
Canaan, 14
Canaanites, the: houses of, 29; religious rites of, 27; temples of, 29; tunnels of, 31
Capernaum, 79, 98
Capitoline Hill, 97

Carbon 14, 5
Carcer Memertinus, 97
Carchemish, 49
Carmel caves (Wadi al-Mugharah), 8
Catacombs, Roman, 66
Cenacle, 82
Cenchreae, 93
Census, of Quirinius, 77
Chagar-Bazar, 17
Chariots, in LB, 19
Chemosh, 37
Cherubim, 33
Chorazin, 80
Church of the Annunciation, 78-79
Church of the Holy Nativity, 78
Church of the Holy Sepulchre, 85
Church of St. Anne, 81
Church of St. Peter Gallicantu, 82
Cilicia, 34, 38, 51
Circus Maximus, 97
Cistern: Herodian, 74, 82; rock, 9
Claudius, 91
Cloaca Maxima, 97
Coffins, Philistine, 28
Coins: Agrippa I, 87; of Bar Kochba, 71; Caesar's, 67; Capernaum, 79; dating, 66; denarius, 67; Greek, 57; Herodian, 66; Jewish, 56, 67, 106; Judaea Capta, 107; Roman, 66
Colosse, 94, 103
Colosseum, 66, 97
Constantine, 78
Corinth, 91-92
Cornelius, 99
Court of Israel, 70
Court of the Women, 70
Covenant, Sinaitic, 23-24
Cremation, 26
Croesus, 102
Crown, athlectic, 93
Crucifixion, 84
Cuneiform: Akkadian, 24, 25; Anatolian, 24; Mesopotamian, 24; Sumerian, 24; Syrian, 24
Cyprus, 14, 28, 53, 54, 89
Cyprus (Khirokitia), 9

Dagan, 27
Daggers, Philistine, 30

113

Damascus, 41, 55, 88-89
Damascus Gate, 105
Dan, in LB, 18
Daniel, 50
Darb al-Mustaqim (Bab Sharqi) Street, 88
Darius I, 56
Darius the Mede, 54
Dating: basis of, 5; stratification and, 5, 7; typology and, 5
David: and Edom, 34; leadership of, 31; and the Philistines, 29, 31; and Saul, 30, 31; structures of, 33
Dead Sea Scrolls, 66, 74-75
Dibir, 29, 35, 51
Deir' Alla, 29
Delos, 80, 98
Delphi, 91
Demeter, 92
Demetrius, 94
Diaspora, 66, 80, 88, 98
Dibhan (Dibon), 8
Didyma, 93
Dilbat, 17
Documents, pre-EB, 15
Dominus Flevit, 87
Domitian, 100, 107
Donkeys, in EB, 18
Dor, 14, 55
Duddiya, 14
Dung Gate, 83
Dura Europos, 80

Ebal, 81
Eber, 14
Ebrum, kingdom of, 14
Edom, 8, 22, 42, 48, 57
Egibi, 56
Egypt: and Assyria, 49; craftsmen of, 51; Hyksos empire, 20; in LB, 18-19; Middle Kingdom (Dynasty XXII), 19; synagogues in, 80
Ekron, 29, 48
Elam, 51
El-Azariyeh, 82
Elephantine papyri, 55
Eliakim, 51
Epic of Gilgamesh, 9, 24
Ephesus, 93-94, 100-1

Erastus, 92
Erech, 15
Eridu, 15
Esarhaddon, 48
Esdraelon, 9
Et-Tell (Ai?), 8
Exodus, date of the, 22
Ezion Geber, 42

Fara, 15
Felix, 95, 104
Festus, 95
Figurines, 18, 26
Flood, Babylonian accounts of, 9
Fortress Antonia, 83
Frescoes, 82

Gadara, 80
Gallio, 91
Gal'za, 42
Gamala, 105
Gate of the Chain, 69
Gath, 14, 28, 44
Gath (Tel el-'Areini or Tell en-Najila?), 29
Gaza, 9, 20, 28, 29, 42, 48, 50
Gealiyah, 25
Gebal, 48
Gedaliah, 26, 52
Gerar, 28
Gerizim, 81
Geshem, 55
Gezer, 14, 15, 27, 29, 31; destruction of, 34; Egyptian defenses at, 35; excavation of, 7; in the exile period, 52; in the Iron Age, 32; and the Maccabees, 58; resettlement of, 55
Ghassul, 9
Gibeah, 29, 35
Gibeah (Tell el-Ful), 30
Gibeon, 31
Giv'at ha-Mivtar, 71, 84, 86
Golden Gate, 69
Gomorrah, 17
Gozan (Guzan, Tell Halaf), 43
Greece, 65; armies of, 57; influence of, 57
Gubaru/Gobryas, 54

General Index

Hadadezer, 38
Hadrian, 72, 74, 77, 78, 84, 95
Haifa, 27
Halah, 43
Hamath, 38, 39, 50
Hammath-Tiberias, 80
Hammurapi, 18
Harran, 49
Hazael, 38
Hazor, 14, 27, 31, 57; bronze objects found at, 34; burning of, 21; destruction of, 42, 44; in the Iron Age, 32; rebuilt by Ahab, 37; temples of, 26
Hebrews, the: economic conditions of, 56; as exiles, 43; and Mesopotamia, 79; and the Philistines, 21, 29; restoration of, 55; languages of Canaan familiar to, 25. *See also* Jews.
Hebron, 49, 74
Hebron (Kirjath-Arba), 17
Hegra, 55
Helena, 84-85
Herculaneum, 96
Herod Agrippa I, 73, 82, 105
Herod Antipas, 76-77, 89
Herodias, 77
Herodium, 74, 105, 106
Herod Philip, 67
Herod the Great, 58, 66, 67, 68
Heshban, 84, 86
Hezekiah, 49; and Assyria, 44, 45, 46
Hierapolis, 94, 103-4
Hieroglyphs, Egyptian, 24, 25
High places, 27, 37
Hippicus, 71
Hippodrome, 73
Hittites, 19
Horses, in LB, 19
Hoshaiah, 51
Hoshea: and Assyria, 42; and Egypt, 44
House of Annas, 82
Houses: in EB, 15; Herodian, 82
Huldah Gates, 69
Hyksos, 19, 20
Hyrcanus I, 75
Hyrcanus, John, 75

Idumea, 57
Inheritance, Nuzi texts concerning, 18

Jaazaniah, 25
Jacob, 18
Jaffa, 55; Gate, 71
Janneus, Alexander, 58
Jarash (Antioch), 57
(Jeho)ahaz, 42
Jehoiachin, 51, 53
Jehoiakim, 25, 50, 51
J(eh)oram, 37
Jehu: and Assyria, 38; and Hazael, 39; and Shalmaneser III, 38
Jericho: destruction of, 15, 21; excavation of, 7; figurines found at, 9; Herodian 73; in MB, 20
Jeroboam I, 35
Jeroboam II, 40
Jerome, 78
Jerusalem, 8, 15; Armenian Quarter, 82; capture of, 51; destruction of, 52, 77; excavation at, 7, 68-69, 85; and Gentile Christians, 78; and Herod, 68; influence of Solomon on, 32-33; Jewish Quarter, 82; model of, 72; Ophel hill, 88; and the Philistines, 29; royal construction of, 40; siege of, 46, 47, 105-6; temple of, 55, 65, 68, 71; Upper City of, 82; walls of, 105; water tunnels of, 45
Jesus Christ: birth of, 77-78; childhood of, 78-79; crucifixion of, 84; tomb of, 84-86; trial of, 83-84
Jews: at Corinth, 92; at Phrygia, 99; revolt of, 104-7; at Sardis, 102. *See also* Diaspora; Hebrews.
Jezebel, 36
Joab, 31
Joash, 39
Johanan, 55, 84
John, the apostle, 100-1
John the Baptist, 76
Jonathan, 30
Joppa, 28
Jordan, 65
Jordan valley, in EB, 9
Joseph, 19
Josephus, 66, 67, 72, 74, 77, 78, 87, 102, 104, 105
Josiah, 49
Jotham, 25

Judah: and Assyria, 44, 48, 49; and Babylon, 50; defeat of, 51-52; and Egypt, 49; and Persia, 55; coinage of, 56
Judas of Galilee, 77, 104
Jugurtha, 97
Justin Martyr, 78
Justinian, 78

Kadesh-Barnea, 52
Karatepe, 33
Karnak, 35
Kassites, 19
Kerti Huyuk, 90
Khirbet Kerak, 15
Khirbet Qumran, 74-75
Khorsabad, 43
Kidron Valley, 82
Kfur Nahum, 79
Kursi, 80-81

Laban, 17
Labynetus, 54
Lachish, 14, 49, 51, 52; deserted, 57; destruction of, 21; excavation of, 47; in the Iron Age, 28; and Rehoboam, 35; resettlement of, 55; siege of, 46, 47; temples of, 26
Lagash, 15
Laodicea, 94, 103
Lazarus, 82
Lu'ash, 39
Lucius Flavius Silva, 107
Lydia, 51, 90, 91
Lydia (country), 102
Lykus, 90
Lysanias, 76
Lystra, 89-90

Maccabees, 57, 58
Maccabeus, Judah, 57
Macedonia, 95
Machaerus, 77, 105, 106
Madeba, 37
Magdala, 80
Malta, 96
Mamre, 74
Manasseh, 40, 48, 49
Mar(Ben)-Yamin (Benjamin), 17

Marduk, 53
Marduk-apla-iddina II, 44
Mari, 39; letters, 18; texts. *See* Texts, Mari.
Mariamne, 71
Marisa, 57, 58
Marriage contracts, 17
Mary Magdalene, 80
Masada, 8, 58, 73-74, 105, 106, 107
Mattaniah-Zedekiah, 51
Mattocks, 30
Mazar, 106
Medes, 49
Media, 51
Medinet Habu, 28
Megiddo: Babylonian occupation of, 53; civilization of, 16; destruction of, 21, 39; in EB I, 14; Egyptian occupation of, 49; excavation of, 7; in the Iron Age, 32; in LB, 20; in MB, 20; stone buildings at, 40; temples of, 26
Megiddo (III): destruction of, 44
Meheleb, 41
Menahem, 40
Mesopotamia (Erbil), 14
Michmash, battle of, 30
Miletus, 95, 98
Mines, at Aqabah, 34
Mirsim, 16
Mizpah, 52
Moab, 22, 42, 48
Moabite Stone, 37
Mosah, 52
Mosque, Al-aksah, 69
Mount of Olives, 87
Mount Scopus, 70
Mount Vesuvius, 96
Mount Zion, 82
Murashu, 56
Musical instruments, 32

Nabateans, culture of the, 57
Nabonidus, 54
Nahalmusur, 41
Naharayah, 27
Nahur (Nahor), 17
Nails, 30
Naram-Sin, 9
Nazareth, 78-79

General Index

Nea Paphos, 89, 105
Neapolis, 78, 90
Nebi Samwil, 52
Nebuchadnezzar, 50, 51, 53, 54, 56
Necho, 56
Necho II, 49
Negeb, 9, 17
Nero, 92, 104
Nicanor, 70
Nile, 9
Nimrod, 9
Nimrud (Calah), 8. *See also* Calah
    (Nimrud)
Nineveh, 8; exploration of, 6; fall of, 49
Nippur, 7, 8, 15
Nomads: Amorite, 15; Palestinian, 16;
    Syro-Palestinian, 14; Trans-
    jordinian, 16
Nubia, 46
Nuzi, 8; texts. *See* Texts, Nuzi.

Octavian, 90
Omri: influence of, 27; palace of, 36;
    and Zimri, 36
Ophel, 31, 33
Ophir, 33
Opis, 53
Origen, 80
Osorkon II, 38
Osorkon IV, 44
Ossuaries, 66, 86-87
Ostia, 99

Paintings, polychrome wall, in the
    Chalcolithic period, 9
Palestine, 14, 65; inscriptions, 25; in
    LB, 18-19, 21
Pallas, 95
Pamukkale, 103
Paphos, 89
Parthenon, the, 66
Patara, 95
Patmos, 100
Patriarchs: and Amorites, 16; in MBA
    I, 16
Paul, the apostle: and Damascus, 88-89;
    first missionary journey of, 89-90;
    imprisonment and burial of, 97-98;
    at Rome, 96-97; second missionary

journey of, 90-93; third missionary
    journey of, 93; and Silas, 90; and the
    synagogue, 88; and Timothy, 90;
    voyage of, to Rome, 95-96
Pekah, 41
Pella, 107
Perga, 89
Pergamum, 91, 101
Persia, 51, 56
Peter, the apostle: home of, 98; ministry
    of, 98; tomb of, 99
Petra, 27, 89
Phasael, 71
Philadelphia, 103
Philip of Iturea, 76
Philippi, 90
Philistia (Ashkelon), 51
Philistines, the: and the Hebrews, 29;
    houses of, 29; origin of, 28; and the
    patriarchs, 28; temples of, 29; and
    Tjekker colonists, 28
Phoebe, 93
Phoenicians, the: as craftsmen, 51;
    influences of, 57; influence of, on the
    Hebrews, 32; and Judah, 55
Pilate, Pontius, 83
Pithom, 21
Ploughshares, 30
Poetry: Egyptian, 34; Mesopotamian,
    34; Syrian, 34
Pollen analysis, 5
Pompeii, 83, 96
Pontius Pilate, 83
Pools, in Jerusalem, 81
Poseidon, 92
Potiphar, 20
Pottery: Chalcolithic, 9; of EB, 15; and
    dating, 5; Edomite, 57; Greek, 57,
    58; of the Iron Age, 28; of MBA-
    LBA, 27; of NT times, 66; Philistine,
    28; Phoenician, 16, 58; Syrian, 16;
    wheel, 16
Praxitiles, 96
"Proto-Hebrew," 25
Ptolemies, 56
Ptolemy II, 57
Ptolemy Philadelphus, 55
Pul(u), 41
Puteoli, 96

117

Qantir, 21
Qarqar, battle of, 38
Qaush(Chemosh)-gabri, 48
Queen of Sheba, 34
Quirinius, 77
Qumran, 8, 58, 66, 74-76; *See also* Texts, Qumran.

Ra'amses, 21
Rachel, 18
Ramat Rachel, 40, 52
Rameses II, 21
Rameses III: tomb of, 28
Rapihu, 44
Ras Shamra, 8, 17, 27, 33: *See also* Texts, Ras Shamra.
Rebekah, 17
Rehoboam, and Egypt, 35
Rezin, 41
Rimah, 39
River Euphrates, 53
Rmat el-Khalil, 74
Rome, 97
Royal Stoa, 91, 106.

Sabbath, 70
St. Stephen's Gate, 70
Salamis, 89
Samaria, 40; controlled by Persia, 55; destruction of, 42; Hellenistic structures of, 57; Jehu's refortification of, 39; occupied by Babylon, 53; and Omri, 36; rebuilt, 71; resettlement of, under Sargon II, 43
Samson, 29
Sanballat, 55
Saqqara, 50
Sarah, 17
Sardis, 94, 102
Sargon II, 43
Sarugi (Serug), 17
Saul, 30
Scriptorium, 75
Sea of Galilee, 79
Sea peoples, 28
Seals: Cretan, 28; in EB, 18; Hebrew, 25; South Arabian stamp, 34; stamp, 25
Sebaste, 71-72

Sebastiyeh (Samaria), 8
Seeia, 67, 76
Seleucids, 56, 57
Semites, alphabet of the, 24-25
Seneca, 91
Sennacherib, 45ff.
Serapis, 92, 101
Sergius Paulus, 89
Sethos I, 21
Settlements, in EB I, 14
Sha'ar Haggolan, 9
Shalmaneser III, 37, 38
Shalmaneser V, 42, 43
Sharezer, 48
Sharuhen, 20, 28, 35
Shebitku, 46
Shechem, 17; Jeroboam's refortification at, 35; in LB, 18; and Omri, 36; temples of, 26
Shema', 25, 40
Shephelah, 28
Shiloh, 29, 30
Shishak, 35, 39
Shrammelech, 48
Siamun, 34
Sib'e, 44
Sibraim, 43
Sickles, 30
Sidon, 41
Silo, grain, in EB, 15
Siloam, pool of, 81
Simon Zelotes, 104
Sinai, 14, 23-24
Slavery: in Egypt, 19; value of, 41
Smyrna, 101
Socrates, 91
Sodom, 17
Sokoh, 49
Solomon: central palace of, 32; and Jerusalem, 32-33; marriage of, 34; stables of, 32; structures of, 32; temple of, 22, 29, 33, 34
Son, first-born, 17
Stela: Aramaic, 39; Egyptian, 20; at Megiddo, 35; of Seti I, 22; Tiglath Pileser's, 41
Street of the Curetes, 94
Sundial, 70
Susa, 7

General Index

Susa Gate, 69
Sychar, 81
Syria, 18-19, 51, 65
Synagogues, 79-80, 88, 98, 99

Ta'anach: excavation of, 7; in the Iron Age, 32
Tainat, 32, 33
Talpioth, 87
Talmud, 78, 82
Tammuz-Adonis, 78
Tanis, 21
Tattanu (Tattenai), 56
Tell Abu Hawam, 55
Tell Arad, 52
Tell Beit Mirsim: destruction of, 21, 47; excavation of, 7; in LB, 18; in MB, 20; occupied by seminomads, 15; walls at, 30, 31
Tell Dan, 27
Tell Dotha (Dothan), 8
TeDuweir(Lachish, 8
Tell el-'Ajjul: Egyptian defenses at, 35; in LB, 18, 20; occupied by seminomads, 16; pottery found at, 28
Tell el-Far'ah (Tirzah), 8; in EBI, 14; in the Iron Age, 35; in LB, 18; pottery found at, 28; resettlement of, 55; temples of, 26
Tell el-Ful (Gibeah), 8
Tell el-Hesi: destruction of, 21; excavation of, 7; in the Iron Age, 32; pottery found at, 28
Tell Hum, 79
Tell el-Husn (Beth-shan), 8
Tell el-Jib (Gibeon), 8
Tell el Kheleifeh, 33
Tell el-Kheleifeh (Ezion-geber, Ezion Geber), 8
Tell el Maskuteh (Succoth), 55
Tell el-Quedar (Hazor), 8
Tell el-Yehudieh, 66
Tell en-Nasbeh: identification of, 52; Jeroboam's refortification of, 35; Philistine wares found at, 29; pottery found at, 15, 49
Tell es-Saidiyeh, 33
Tell Halaf (biblical Gozan), 32
Tell Hariri (Mari), 8

Tell Jemmeh, Egyptian defenses at, 35
Tell Mor, destruction of, 34
Tell Mardikh, excavations at, 9
Tell Qasileh, 8, 29, 33
Tell Seilun (Shiloh), 8
Tell Sheikh el-Areini (Gath), 8
Tell Shuneh, in EB I, 14
Telulot Ghassul, 9
Tema', 54
Temple in Jerusalem. See Jerusalem, temple of.
Temples, in the Bronze Age, 26
Texts: Akkadian, 6, 31; Assyrian, 6, 37; Aramaic, 23; Babylonian, 6, 37, 51; cuneiform, 23; Hittite, 24; Hurrians, 24; Mari, 17, 31, Nuzi, 17, 18; Qumran, 31; Ras Shamra, 17; Sumerian, 6, 24; Ugarit, 24, 27
Thessaloniac, 91
Thyatira, 90, 101-2
Tiberius, 67, 76, 95
Tidal (Tudhalia), 18
Tiglath Pileser, 41, 42
Tigris valley (Jarmo), 9
Timnah, 29
Tirhaka, 46, 48
Tirzah: in LB, 18; and Omri, 36
Tirzah (II), destruction of, 44
Titus, 77, 105, 107
Tobiad, 55, 57
Tomb of the Kings, 86
Tombs: in EB, 16; at Jericho, 16; in MB IIC, 19; at Megiddo, 16; at Mesopotamia, 16; at Ras Shamra, 16; at Tell el-'Ajjul, 16; at Tell el-Fara'ah, 30
Towns, in EB, 14-15
Treaties: Esarhaddon Assyrian, 23; Hittite, 23
Troas, 95
Troy, 90
Tubingen school, 63
Tudia, 14
Tullianum, 97
Tunnels, water, 31
Turahi (Terah), 17
Turkey, 89

Ugarit: scripts, 25; temples, 26

Ur, 7, 8, 15, 17
Urusalem (Jerusalem), 14
Ushtannu, 56
Uzziah, 40

Vercingetorix, 97
Vespasian, 95, 105
Via Egnatia, 91

Wadi Qelt, 73
Wailing Wall, 69
Warehouses, 73, 93
Warka, 7, 8
Wen-Amun, 25
Widiya, 28
Wilbur Papyri, 19
Wilson's Arch, 69

Yamani, 44
Yaosh, 51

Ya'qub-il (Jacob), 17
Yarmuk, 9
Yathrib (Medina), 54
Yaudi, 40
Ya'usu (Joash), 39
Yodefat, 105

Zabilan (Zebulon), 17
Zakir, 39
Zaphenath-Paneah, 20
Zarethan, 33
Zedekiah, 51
Zeno, 55
Zerubbabel, 68
Zincirli, 32
Zion Gate, 83
Ziph, 49

SCRIPTURE INDEX

Genesis
5 15
10 15
10:9 9
10:11-12 8
10:21 14
14 18
15:4 17
18:7 17
20 17
20:1 17
21:10ff. 17
23 18
24:62 17
26 17
26:12 17
29:18 17
29:27 17
34:12 17
37-50 19
37:7 17
37:28 19
41:14 20
48:14ff. 17

Exodus
1:11 21
1:15 19
20:2 23
20:31 23
25:16 23
27:1 34

Numbers
13:28 19
26:29-33 40

Deuteronomy
1:1-5 23
1:6-3:29 23
10:1-5 23
28 23
31:10-13 23

Joshua
6:26 26
11 21
21:26 52

Judges
1:18 21
1:31 41
3:31 29
14:4 29
14:11-12 29
16:29 29
16:30 29

1 Samuel
8:11-18 19
13:3 30
13:14 30
18-22 30
27:6 19

2 Samuel
5:6-8 31

1 Kings
6:1 22
7:45 33
8:65 33
9:15 32
10:28 34
12:25 36
14:25-26 35
15:15-22 35
16:21-28 37
16:31 36
22:38 37
22:39 37

2 Kings
1:1 37
3:27 37
10:32 39

13:14-19 39
13:24 39
13:25 39
15:5 40
15:19ff. 41
15:30ff. 25
15:37 41
16:5-9 41
16:8 42
16:10-16 42
17:3-6 42
17:4 44
17:24 44
18:10 43
18:18 26
19:9 46
19:37 47
20:20 45
23:29 49
24:7 52
24:10-17 51
24:17 51
25:23-25 53
25:23 26

1 Chronicles
3:22 25
7:14-19 40
22:3 30

2 Chronicles
6:13 34
32:30 45
36:10 51

Ezra
1:2-4 54
5:3 56
5:6 56
6:6 56
6:13 56

Nehemiah
6:1.................................55
12:22............................55
12:23............................55

Psalms
122:1............................85

Isaiah
7:1ff.............................41
7:9................................42
9:11..............................41
13..................................43
29:11-12.......................33
37:9..............................46
37:38............................48
59:12............................33

Jeremiah
6:1................................51
7:12..............................31
29:9-1...........................50
34:7..............................52
36:1-9...........................50
40:5..............................52
40:8..............................53
49:28-33........................50
50:38............................53

Ezekiel
9:4................................87
44:1-2...........................69
47:16............................43

Daniel
4:30..............................53
6:28..............................54

Amos
6:4................................37
8:11..............................39

Matthew
8:28..............................80
11:20-21........................80
22:19-21........................67

23:2..............................80
23:5..............................80
24:1ff...........................104
26:57............................82
27:57-60........................86
28:12-13........................86

Mark
1:21..............................79
5:1................................80
7:11..............................70
13:1......................68, 104
15:7.............................104
15:21............................88

Luke
2:2................................77
2:8-18...........................78
3:1................................76
4:31-37.........................79
6:15.............................104
8:26..............................80
15:8-9...........................67
21:5ff..........................104

John
2:20..............................68
4:20..............................81
5....................................81
9:7................................81
18:1..............................82
18:13............................82
19:1..............................84
19:13............................84
19:31-32........................84
20:27............................84

Acts
2:5-11...........................98
2:10..............................99
5:37......................77, 104
6:9................................88
9:11..............................88
10:1..............................99
12:21-23........................73
13:7..............................89

13:13-14........................89
14:12............................89
16:12............................90
16:13............................91
16:14...........................104
17:6..............................91
17:23............................91
18:12-17........................91
19:22............................92
19:24ff..........................94
19:29-31........................94
20:13............................95
21:8.............................104
21:27-30........................70
21:38...........................104
27:7..............................96
28:7..............................96
28:13............................96

Romans
16:1..............................93
16:23............................92

1 Corinthians
9:25..............................93
15:33............................94

2 Corinthians
11:32............................89

Ephesians
2:4................................70

Colossians
4:13.............................103

1 Peter
1:1................................98

Revelation
1:9...............................100
2–3..............................100
2:13.............................101
3:16.............................103
3:18.............................103